LANDSCAPES
OF CYCLING

LANDSCAPES
OF CYCLING

GRAHAM WATSON

BOULDER, COLORADO

Printed in China
10 9 8 7 6 5 4 3 2 1
Distributed in the United States and Canada by Publishers
Group West.

Jacket and interior design: Elizabeth M. Watson

Library of Congress Cataloging-in-Publication Data
Watson, Graham.
    Landscapes of cycling / Graham Watson.
        p. cm.
    Includes index.
    ISBN 1-931382-48-4 (hardcover : alk. paper)
    1. Photography of sports. 2. Landscape photography. 3.
Cycling—Pictorial works. 4. Bicycling—Pictorial works. I. Title.

TR821.W3824 2004
779'.97966'2—dc22   2004013874

VeloPress®
1830 North 55th Street
Boulder, Colorado 80301–2700 USA
303/440-0601 · Fax 303/444–6788
E-mail velopress@insideinc.com

To purchase additional copies of this book or other VeloPress®
books, call 800/234-8356 or visit us on the Web at velopress.com.

FRONT COVER: The Passo Sella straddles one of Italy's most
beautiful roads, which forms one of the most famous
climbs in cycling. But it comes just a few kilometers after
the more beautiful and famous Passo di Gardena, thus
creating a challenge for the landscape photographer.
Stay too long on the Gardena climb and you'll be stuck
behind the race until after the descent of the Sella.
Experiences—yes, bad ones—have taught me to speed
away on the motorbike in the last kilometer of the
Gardena in order to get to the Sella summit in time to
change film and get my act together for a shot like this.
Camera: Nikon F5; lens: 28–80mm zoom; film: 50asa Velvia;
exposure: 1/320@f6.3

◀ I consider the Passo Val Gardena the prettiest cycling climb in the world. In 1993 the weather was absolutely perfect for landscape photography, and the Giro d'Italia peloton acted with equal perfection to stay together for the entire climb. For me, this is a timeless image of the Giro in the Dolomites, with rocky spires towering over the tiny cyclists to create a fantastic skyline. The ground is still green enough in early June to offer the perfect foreground . . . absolutely perfect.
Camera: Nikon F4;
lens: 16mm fisheye;
film: 50asa Velvia;
exposure: 1/250@f5.6

▶ Acres of sunflowers surrounded the eighth stage of the Tour de France in 2000. This is an extremely rare shot, as the flowers are in full bloom, but not yet bleached by the sun as is normal in mid-July. It is also unusual to happen across so many sunflowers in one place. In addition, the fields were banked away from the road, giving photographers the perfect angle.
Camera: Nikon F5;
lens: 300mm;
film: 100asa;
exposure: 1/320@f5.6

CONTENTS

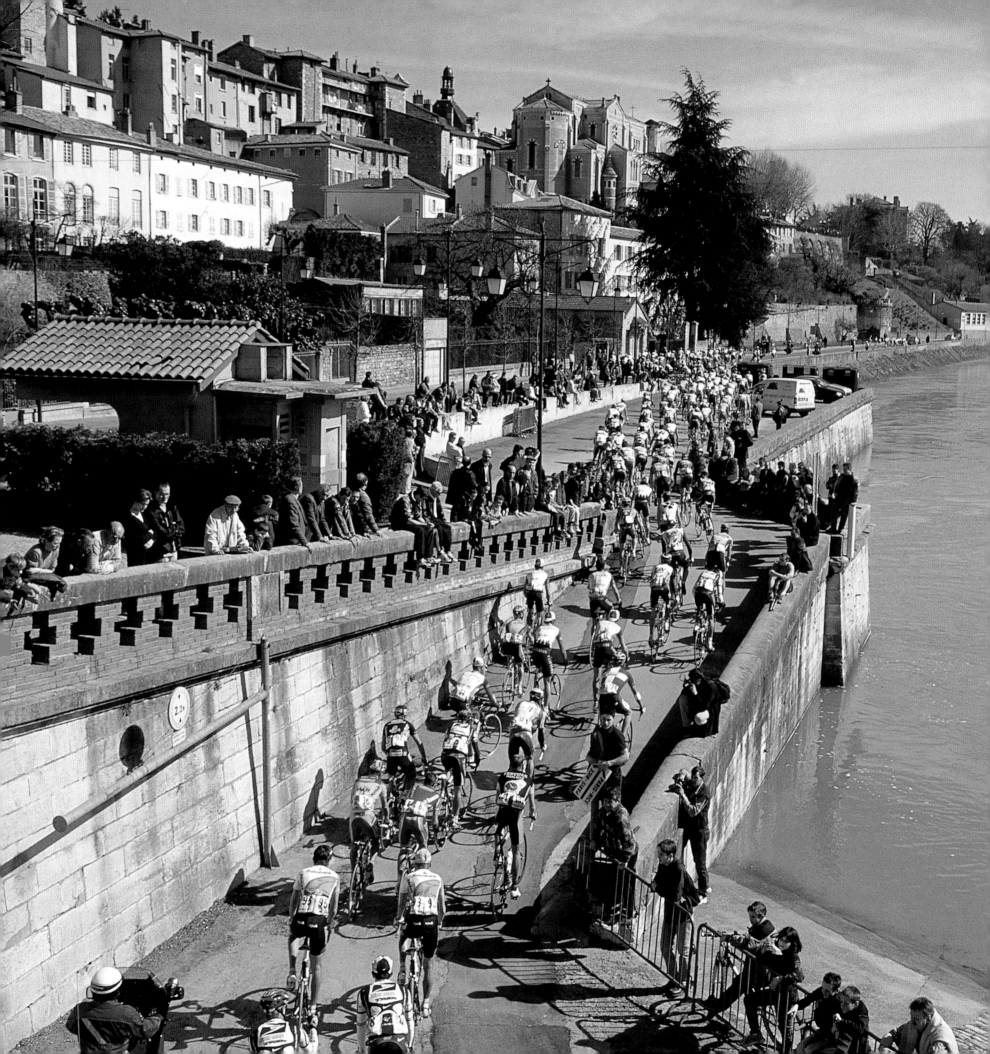

FOREWORD

The beauty of cycling lies not only in the ever-changing kaleidoscope of the race, but also in the infinitely varied landscapes through which it travels. These landscapes are not mere backdrops. They give a race its character and even influence its unfolding character. A tight bend in the road here, a narrow bridge there, a sharp climb up a city street, or a stretch of cobblestones through the open countryside: Any of these features can inspire a tactical move, instigate a crash, or cause a split in the peloton. It's photographer Graham Watson's job to identify these key moments and then shoot them.

Graham witnesses the world's leading bike races from the back of a motorcycle, and this mobility enables him to pick the locations he deems important to truly capture an event's character. The landscapes are perhaps the hardest images of all to capture because the photographer has such a tiny window of opportunity.

A bike race is always on the move. To take an action shot, Graham takes his turn with other motorcycle-mounted photographers to drift back from their position ahead of the peloton and ride alongside the racers. That stuff is relatively easy. But if he decides to photograph a landscape, he has to motor ahead of the race, look for a good angle from which to shoot it, find the ideal place to stand, and then get just a second or two to take the photo as the race passes through his viewfinder. Then, he and his driver have to work their way through the race, past the peloton, and take up their position again at the front—hoping that no vital moves have been made in their absence.

Graham is so good at finding the great landscapes and angles because he had a long apprenticeship, using his own bicycle, then his own car, to get around races from the outside, before finally graduating to a motorcycle inside the race. I remember working an early-season race with him in France, the Étoile de Bessèges, when he stood on my shoulders to get a

◄ The picturesque town of Romans-sur-Isére on the banks of the Isére was a most idyllic setting for the start of a Paris-Nice stage in 1999. This is another example of how a colorful bike race completes an already picturesque scene, yet the race does not overpower the image—it merely complements the scenery.
Camera: Nikon F5; lens: 80–200mm zoom; film: 50asa Velvia; exposure: 1/250@f6.3

higher angle for a shot of the peloton emerging from a double line of plane trees. One day at the Tour de France in the Normandy town of Pont-Audemer, I spotted Graham standing in the upstairs window of a half-timbered medieval house, waiting to shoot a fast-moving line of riders crossing the cobblestone square.

Now that he attends more bike races than perhaps any other photographer, Graham is always searching out new angles. In March 2004, for example, I saw him shoot the peloton crossing the Meuse River at the Critérium International, pointing his wide-angle lens into the sun to get a better impression of the early morning mist rising from the water. Then, at April's Liège-Bastogne-Liège classic, he scampered up a grassy hillside to find the best angle to shoot a breakaway group as it raced past an onion-domed church in the Ardennes. And at May's Tour de Romandie, he achieved the rare combination of shooting the race ascending a green, green valley just as Tyler Hamilton's Phonak team was putting on the pressure and splitting apart the peloton.

Photographically, Graham can do everything just right, but he still has to hope that the sun comes out when he needs it, or that the rain will stop before ruining his shot. The landscapes he chose for this book include the lucky shots as well as the ones that are technically perfect. In the end, they say as much about Graham and his skills as they do about the races themselves. It's a beautiful sport, and Graham's photography has helped it become just that much more beautiful.

John Wilcockson

Author and *VeloNews* Editorial Director

◄ This was a lucky shot completely, yet it still brings me satisfaction. . . . We were following the peloton down a narrow climb in the Ardeche in the 2004 Paris-Nice, when suddenly this bridge came into view 1,000 feet below us—and the race was going to cross it! I stopped at the first available overlook and managed to snap a series of images before the speeding cyclists crossed the bridge and disappeared in just a few seconds. I'm not sure what makes this image—the glare off the water or the ant-like cyclists picking their way across the bridge.
Camera: Nikon D2H; lens: 300mm; digital image rated 200asa; exposure: 1/500@6.3

ACKNOWLEDGMENTS

I like to think I have something of a photographic memory. . . . While I have managed to remember most of the places and locations illustrated in this book, I've also had to call upon a small group of friends and colleagues in order to confirm or change any questionable facts herein. To identify a certain village in Tuscany, a chateau in the Loire Valley, a remote Alp in France, or an exposed moor in northern England is one thing. But to then have to ascertain whether it was taken at the 1988 Tour of Ireland, the 1986 Tour of Spain, or the 1981 Paris-Nice required a great deal of research and questioning. So to these people: John Wilcockson, Jacky Koch, Christian Biville, Roberto Bettini, Stephen Farrand, and Graham Jones—a big thank you! Inevitably, there will still be gaps in my knowledge and that of my advisors, so I must offer a big apology to anyone offended by any such errors—I'm only human after all!

▶ The north of England is where most of Britain's best roadmen have come from—and it is hardly surprising given the tough hills of Lancashire, Yorkshire, and Derbyshire. Here we are in Yorkshire, passing over a quaint bridge in the heart of the county. This part of the world is comparatively underpopulated, so the only spectators on this day were hundreds of bemused sheep.
Camera: Nikon F4; lens: 180mm; film: 100asa;
exposure: 1/500@f4

INTRODUCTION

Imagine a flowing peloton of cyclists racing up an alpine road against a stunning backdrop of fir trees, crystal-clear lakes, and towering, snowy peaks that pierce a deep blue sky. Then picture another pack of cyclists riding between acres and acres of sunflowers in central France, their multicolored jerseys in perfect harmony with the intense yellow of their surroundings. Now envision a third group of racers bumping across a cobbled back road that follows the contours of a hill historically known for its strategic role in World War I. If you can imagine photographing these sights as a daily vocation, you may begin to appreciate how much I love my work as a cycling photographer.

To say I fell in love with the sport of cycling so many years ago would be the understatement of my life. As a 21-year-old enthusiast, I went to Paris to see the end of the 1977

◄ ◄ The Picos de Europa tower over a group of cyclists in the 1990 Vuelta a España as they arrive at a stage finish in Lagos de Covadonga. It was quite a hike up the hillside to capture this view, but now—nearly ten years after the Vuelta spoiled its beauty by moving to September—I'm very glad that I made the effort.
Camera: Bronica ETRs; lens: 75mm; film: 50asa Velvia; exposure: 1/500@f5.6–f8

◄ This is the Kellogg's Tour of Britain in 1991, climbing Kirkstone Pass in the Lake District—England's most treasured region. In the background is Lake Windermere, but this is clearly an overcast day in England, so for now just try to appreciate the lush greenery and come back another time.
Camera: Nikon F4; lens: 85mm; film: 100asa; exposure: 1/250@f4

Tour de France—and found both my passion and my future. From then on, I was determined to experience as much of this beautiful sport as I could. So I cycled my way around France on more than one entire Tour, climbed many of the sport's greatest mountains, and saw panoramas that were the stuff of dreams. My quest was simple: to wring every bit of pleasure out of my great adventure before the day it would inevitably end. Except it never *did* end . . . and almost thirty years later I'm still seeking out those same adventures, still climbing those grand old mountains and new ones as well, and experiencing a never-ending love affair with cycling.

It is the landscapes that evoke my passion, as they have from the start. The racers? They come and go, a harsh fact of life I learned quickly, watching heroes like Sean Kelly, Phil Anderson, and Bernard Hinault retire, just as I was getting my professional "training wheels." But the landscapes never left; they only got better. After my adolescent Tour experience, I went to Spain and the Vuelta a España, and then on to the Giro d'Italia. I was drawn to races like the Ruta del Sol, the Mediterranean Tour, Paris-Nice, the Vuelta a Murcia, Vuelta Valenciana, Semana Catalana, and Tour de Romandie. I even found a keen pleasure in the brutal classics of Belgium and northern France, discovering hidden landscapes amid the cobblestone bleakness of these two war-torn countries, where the racing was so intense that it seemed like one more bloody battle.

As the years passed, I met and embraced many new heroes, and several of them have since become my friends. But while the racing milestones of those great men soon start to fade, it is the immortal landscapes that I return to time and again.

Back in 1979, my panniers bulging with camping and camera gear, I pedaled my way up the Col du Galibier, to choose an exquisite panorama where I could look down on the Tour de France as it wound its way up to us. For sure, I wanted that pin-sharp, in-your-face shot of Bernard Hinault or Joop Zoetemelk as he inched into view, but it was the bigger picture that I was also after: the view across the Alps toward the hidden peak of Mont Blanc, forever shrouded in cloud but there nonetheless. If in '79 it was the Galibier, then in 1980 it was the Alpe d'Huez, in 1981 the Col du Tourmalet, and in 1982 the Col du Glandon. On it went

► The Koppenberg is a legendary landmark on the Tour of Flanders route and a favorite subject for many photographers of cycling's greatest landscapes throughout the years. It fell into disrepair after its exclusion from the race in 1988, but was then excavated and rebuilt in time for the 2002 Tour of Flanders. Hearing of its renovation, I hurried to Belgium, to the hamlet of Melden, to see the Koppenberg one last time before cosmetic surgery removed its startling cobblestones. It was a beautiful winter afternoon and I was the only person to be found on the hill, happily snapping away with my camera until the light died completely. The result was a bit like one of those old Flemish landscapes: poplar trees on a tall horizon with the clear blue sky accentuating the stark beauty of this land.
Camera: Nikon F5; lens: 20–35mm; film: 50asa Velvia; exposure: 1/125@f5.6

until the day when I went beyond France and discovered breathtaking landscapes in Spain, Italy, and Switzerland as well. And not just in the mountains, for there were landscapes to be found in all kinds of terrain.

In the 1970s, I followed only two to three weeks of racing a year, shooting the Tour and a classic or two. These days, established beyond reason and a million miles away from riding a bicycle to access those wonderful mountains, I watch about 160 days of racing in a year—and still cannot get enough! But only a madman could see that much racing and want to capture only those brave cyclists, day in, day out. My working day is based around the *need* to photograph these heroes in action—when they win, when they fall, when they cry, and when they dance merrily on the podium. But my dream, my passion, is to venture far, far away from the racing and discover panoramas never before seen in cycling magazines or books. Yes, it has been an intense pleasure shooting images of Lance Armstrong in his quest to become the first man to win six Tours de France. But even on those most exciting of days, I've still had one eye turned toward the fields alongside the race route, searching for something special with which to remember that day.

Photographing landscapes is an addictive vocation, since you are always looking to better the last image you took. This addiction becomes an all-consuming challenge when you try to compose the "perfect" landscape around an active group of cyclists—for they can either make or break your precious shot, and it's generally the latter! Too many cyclists huddled

▲ The fifth stage of the 2004 Paris-Nice took the race out of the Massif Central and down toward the warmer lands of Provence at Rasteau. It afforded us with views such as this small reservoir near the Col de Prevenchéres in the high Ardeche, where the CSC team was controlling the racing. This region of France is especially remote and quite unknown to outsiders—which is why I like it so much.
Camera: Nikon D2H; lens: 28–80mm; digital image rated 200asa; exposure: 1/500@f6.3

◄ This shot of the Colle di Agnello is one of the most satisfying images I've ever taken. Yet I thought the shot had been lost when the mists blew in across the Alps in the 2000 Giro d'Italia, blocking a superb vista across to Monte Viso. I was about to move on to another location higher up the Agnello when I suddenly saw the mists dissipate, and a haunting mountain peak came into view. It was gone in an instant, and this is the only frame I managed to fire off—there is a ghostly color in the sky, which makes the landscape even more beguiling.
Camera: Nikon F5; lens: 80–200mm; film: 50asa Velvia; exposure: 1/320@f5.6

together and too close to the camera can detract from the landscape, the colors of their jerseys too strong a contrast against a deep green meadow. Yet too few cyclists, or a peloton that has inconsiderately strung itself out into a long line, can make the landscape seem empty or lacking in depth. The backdrop must be just so, the road below you of compositional perfection, and as for the light . . . well, you can sense the challenge.

So, you might ask, why do I persist in shooting landscapes whose success depends on an erratic human element? Simply because I can think of no more perfect image than one that combines a bunch of colorful cyclists and a landscape of mountains or ocean or meadow. Not only do both subjects bring their own distinct beauty, but each enhances the other through the striking contrast of stillness and action.

Whenever I discover an extraordinary panorama ahead of the race, I feel as if I've suddenly become a painter—albeit one with a camera and light meter—trying to create a scene exactly the way I want it, regardless of the many factors and variables that can so easily ruin my imagined tapestry. And it can take years to get it right! In 1987 I composed a majestic overview of the Giro d'Italia as the men climbed into the Dolomites, only to have the sun dip behind some clouds just as the peloton cycled by. I made a mental note of that exact spot, hoping that the next time the Giro went that same way, the sky would be clear and the sun would shine with clarity. Yet that might not happen for years. Similarly, there was a time in Asturias when the light was perfect and the scenery indescribable, but the peloton arrived ripped to bits by some unanticipated racing. I would go back to that same lush valley some years later, hoping that my tapestry finally could be completed.

It's a scenario I've played out many times in many different situations, and I've yet to experience full satisfaction. Perhaps that's one reason why my profession remains so exciting: an endless quest for the grail of the perfect shot. And perhaps that's also why it has taken me the best part of thirty years to compile the images found inside this little book. Meanwhile, I am grateful for my vocation and for the images, and I hope that these landscapes of cycling will give you as much enjoyment as they have generously given me.

▶ The multinational peloton as seen at the 2003 world championships in Hamilton, Ontario. I shot this from a bridge overlooking the course. In fact, I tried the same shot on each of the four road races that took place in Canada. This is the elite men's race, the one with the biggest and most compact peloton, and therefore, it is the one that gave me the best image. There's an annoying gap between rider No.17 (Michael Rogers) and rider No.7 (Paolo Bettini), but other than that, I got the effect I wanted—a different kind of landscape. Camera: Nikon D1X; lens: 300mm; digital image at 200asa; exposure: 1/320@f5.6

WINTER

Hiver, invierno, inverno . . . Winter. For those who live in the Northern Hemisphere, including a Brit like myself, winter appears to be the longest, harshest, and least desirable of the four seasons. November is traditionally the wettest month, December the gloomiest, and January the coldest.

◄ There will never be a more appropriate landscape for winter cycling! The 2001 world cyclo-cross championships took place in Poprad, Slovakia, forty-eight hours after I returned from Australia's Tour Down Under . . . with a temperature change of 40 degrees Centigrade. Nevertheless, Poprad was one of the most spectacular settings for the championships that I've ever known, and the brutal chill was nearly forgotten when scenic shots like this were up for grabs . . . if your film did not break apart inside the camera.
Camera: Nikon F5; lens: 20–35mm; film: 50asa Velvia; exposure: 1/500@f5.6

► Nothing quite beats the colorful blend of a packed peloton riding between long avenues of plane trees in the south of France—especially in the early season, when the spectacle is fresh to the eye. At the Étoile de Bessèges in 2003, the sun is an important factor too, lighting the backs of the cyclists and the wide tree trunks at the same time.
Camera: Nikon F5; lens: 80–200mm; film: 100asa Provia; exposure: 1/500@f6.3

Only February offers any degree of comfort, with its lighter mornings and the first true rays

of a warming sun.

Yet ironically, in this darkest of seasons, the travelling cycling photographer is rewarded

with the year's greatest variety of lighting locations, which change dramatically as you move

around the world. There's the darkness and mystery of a six-day race in Ghent or Grenoble,

the churned-mud delight of a cyclo-cross shot in overcast or snowy Switzerland, the exquisite

South Pacific glare at Australia's Tour Down Under, and the bleakly illuminated world 'cross

▲ Some cyclo-cross races take place in dramatic surroundings, with a mountain backdrop or even an ocean view in some instances. But in Lembeek in 1986, there was only mud—and it seemed like glorious mud to this photographer! It seemed I photographed less of the race and more of the muddy landscape at the time, but I was pleased with this view of an amateur cyclist struggling through the fields. The complete lack of direct light makes this shot even moodier, though it was a difficult one to expose properly.
Camera: Nikon F3; lens: 180mm; film: 100asa pushed to 200asa; exposure: 1/250@f4

▶ The Tour Down Under race in South Australia opened my eyes to the beauty of this continent, or at least one small corner of it! One of the region's most famous landmarks is a bumpy road in Seppeltsfield, in the heart of the Barossa Valley wine region, where a long line of palm trees allowed me to frame the race in its unique environment. What possibly makes this shot, apart from the use of a fisheye lens, is the tiny speck of cloud in the center of the deep blue sky. Every year the race goes back along the same stretch of road, and every year I am compelled to record its beauty, but I have yet to find anything that satisfies me as much as this original shot taken in 1999.

Camera: Nikon F5; lens: 16mm fisheye; film: 50asa Velvia; exposure: 1/320@f6.3

championships held in the brutal chill of Slovakia. Yes, winter offers it all. And surprisingly, it's the brighter, cheerier February that might disappoint the photographer, with a light that's often too white to do anything other than ruin your shot. That changes, of course, if your race starts early enough or dawdles long enough for you to benefit from the two extremes of morning and evening light.

Winter has an added appeal for those of us who cannot get enough of cycling and travelling at a time when most folks are confined to their homes and huddled 'round a fire, or secluded on sun-drenched beaches way below the equator. Safe in the knowledge that for two weeks of this season I, too, will be heading down south, I launch into November with an eye steadfastly focused on the muddy faces that so distinguish cyclo-cross from all other forms of road bike races. Roaming through a boggy Flanders field, or a lush green pasture above the Bay of Biscay, or a cow-trodden meadow in Switzerland, I seek out the winter-pale faces of men whose names are etched into local folklore, hoping to frame riders like

▲ The Australians are a patriotic bunch, even those who hail from England! Every year this elderly couple wheels out their vintage car to watch the Tour Down Under pass through the area of Hahndorf. This is the one stage of the race that is not terribly pretty, so it is nice to capture some of the local characters to add interest alongside landscapes of the sea and desert.

Camera: Nikon F5; lens: 20–35mm; film: 50asa Velvia; exposure: 1/320@f5.6

Zweifel, Stamsnijder, Liboton, Wellens, Di Tano, De Bie, and Thaler within their home landscapes of Zarautz, Diegem, Valkenswaard, Wetzikon, and Brno.

The indoor world of six-day racing fills the same calendar months as cyclo-cross, yet it couldn't offer a greater contrast. Six-day races are staged figuratively and literally in shadowy velodromes, and the six-day arena offers its own unique character to the ever-hopeful photographer. But in truth, only one stadium—Munich's—holds any potential for a true landscape:

◄ This is a rare view of the Tour Mediterranean, one of France's most popular "training" races, held in February, as it was taken in Italy in 2003! We were heading toward the hilltop town of Cervo, slightly east of Imperia, on a looping stage based near Lagueglia. This image is unusual for yet another reason: We pass this same scene in Milan–San Remo just five weeks later, only we are headed in the opposite direction at speeds considerably higher than the Mediterranean race.
Camera: Nikon F5; lens: 80–200mm; film: 100asa Provia; exposure: 1/500@f5.6

► Roundhay Park in Leeds was the scene for the 1992 world cyclo-cross championships, and it was a chance for the British public to put on a great show for the "foreign" visitors, who knew precious little about the enthusiasm we had for cyclo-cross in those days. There was but one chance to show the enormity of the crowds, and as luck would have it, it was also an opportunity to capture an unusual landscape with the medieval gates of Roundhay Castle.
Camera: Nikon F4; lens: 180mm; film: 100asa pushed to 400asa; exposure: 1/250@f4

The Olympiahalle is capacious enough to dwarf the small 285-meter oval and allows you to walk high into the arena's rafters to capture a real gem of an image. The Ghent-Six is another old favorite for this sometimes travel-weary Brit, as it's just a few hours' drive from London on a wintry November day, when the boats and trains are just beginning to fill with early Christmas shoppers stocking up on cheap tobacco and booze. Still, there's no escaping the crowds once you get into Belgium, for booze is the top-selling commodity in the Sportpaleis in Ghent, which guarantees a good turnout of spectators every night of the week. But if you

▼ The Swiss-hosted world cyclo cross-championships in 1988 were made memorable by the amount of rain and snow that fell on the course throughout the weekend, eliminating our views of the nearby mountains. However, it gave us photographers a chance to shoot another form of landscape, one with a distinctly human element. I captured Beat Breu in my sights at a point in the race when he was visibly tiring, looking like a forlorn victim of the thick, oozing mud he was trying so hard to conquer. Camera: Nikon F3; lens: 300mm; film: 100asa pushed to 200asa; exposure: 1/250@f2.8

◄ Although Andalucía is famous for its beaches and vast olive groves, few people realize how mountainous it is. This shot frames the 1993 Ruta del Sol against a backdrop that includes the high snowfields. The area inland from Málaga and Almeria can be quite cold in mid-February, and it is often early April before the snow completely melts away.
Camera: Nikon F4; lens: 135mm; film: 100asa; exposure: 1/500@f4

go there on a Friday or Saturday night, not even the cleverest of lens filters can help your camera record much through the haze and stench created by thousands of smokers and drinkers.

In terms of geography and just about everything else, Australia's Tour Down Under couldn't seem farther away from the six-day circuit even if it were on another planet! And that's exactly where I *feel* I am each January, staggering from the intensity of the light, reeling drunkenly from the sudden shift to a temperature that's 60 degrees Fahrenheit higher than northern Europe's, and gazing at birds, animals, and terrain like you find nowhere else on this earth. Australia defies description. This huge and amazing continent challenges the photographer with the breadth, depth, and diversity of its beauty. It seems like a gift from heaven that some clever bloke decided to

▶ The snows of Sierra Nevada are typically only visible from afar during the Ruta del Sol. But in 1993 there was a stage finish at nearly 3,000 meters among the skiers! Luckily for everyone, it was a warm day, and I cherished the rare opportunity to capture such a gorgeous combination of color—fresh snow, vivid cycling jerseys, tanned legs—and a great race as well.
Camera: Nikon F4; lens: 28–80mm; film: 50asa Velvia; exposure: 1/250@f6.3

put on a bike race there for me to come and photograph in the winter. The only downside of Down Under is that I return to Europe each year wondering where on earth I can capture similarly evocative landscapes.

Set in South Australia, rather than the more populated states of Victoria and New South Wales, the tour reveals the stark beauty of what this continent basically is: a desert. Yet by starting and ending in the Mediterranean-like city of Adelaide, surrounded by vineyard-laden hills and enticingly empty beaches, it offers the perfect antidote to the end-of-winter harshness awaiting me back home. Thank you, Australia, for this seasonal gift. And a special thanks to Joseph Seppelt, who had the wisdom more than a century ago to plant palm trees along a ridge in the Barossa Valley. Good on yer, mate!

Ah, on to Poprad, Koksijde, Gieten, Tabor, Middlefart . . . brrr. European towns with names that can only sound cold greet me on my return from Down Under for the world cyclo-cross championships. But this blight aside, February is also the month in which I swap Aussie sunshine for that of the *real* Mediterranean, specifically southern France and Spain, where a micro-season of "training races" is held each year. Training, they are not. Racing, they are. Yet the racing is mild enough for the first few weeks to allow the photographer to venture far ahead of the race and seek out precious scenic shots. And they're there in abundance! France's treasures include long avenues of plane trees in the Cévennes region, naked vignes along the Rhône Valley, and glorious ocean views on the Côte d'Azur. Then in Spain you can revel in the olive kingdom of Andalucía, the orange grove paradise of Valencia, and the rugged cliffs of the Costa Blanca.

I first went to Andalucía in 1985 for the Ruta del Sol. When I arrived late at night in Málaga, a mate jokingly challenged me to stay awake during the leisurely race by counting how many olive trees I could see on any given stage. It took me just a few moments on the first day to appreciate his humor, for the road between Cabra and Jaén contained about 140 kilometers of unrelenting olive groves . . . an all-too-perfect backdrop for the landscape photographer in winter.

◄ Whether you view Andalucía from the comfort of a car, the side of the road, or even an airplane landing into Málaga, it is always a stunning sight. Seen from a motorbike travelling a few meters behind the Ruta del Sol peloton, the result is unique. We were travelling south toward Benalmadena from Baeña in 2000 when I spotted this image beginning to take shape, a single moment when the rear of the peloton came into total harmony with the mystical mountains. It's almost reminiscent of an Arabian landscape, and there is not a single olive tree in sight.
Camera: Nikon F5; lens: 28–70mm; film: 50asa Velvia; exposure: 1/320@f5.6

◄ The town of Jumilla in the most northerly part of Murcia is the backdrop for this shot of the 2001 Vuelta a Murcia. I had to travel a long way ahead of the race to spot this, and I did so purely by accident: I was looking for a head-soothing cup of coffee after drinking too many glasses of the rich red wine originating from Jumilla's little-known vineyards. But the ingredients were there for a nice landscape: a compact peloton inching its way toward me as the town's ancient fortress hovered over the whole scene. The race cars have slightly impaired our view, but not enough to spoil a truly unusual shot that I'm proud to have taken.

Camera: Nikon F5;
lens: 300mm;
film: 100asa Provia;
exposure: 1/250@f3.5

◀ The Vuelta a la Comunidad Valenciana passes by a
typical mountain village in 2000. This shot survived an
unlucky moment when the sun went behind a cloud just
as the race came by. But the fact that the peloton is the
one element in the shadows safeguards the focal point of
this landscape: the hilltop village, which remains bathed
in glorious sunshine. In fact, the cyclists become more
foreground than focal point, but this image might not
work at all if the peloton was also bathed in sunshine . . .
there would be too many contradicting factors to
deal with.
Camera: Nikon F5; lens: 20–35mm; film: 50asa Velvia;
exposure: 1/320@f5

▶ The G.P. Marseillaise is a one-day race that opens the
French cycling season each year, and it is nearly always
based on circuits around the busy market town of
Aubagne, where a small hill above the town serves as
the perfect finish. Three times up the hill means three
times past this picturesque church and a chance to make
full use of the lighting. In the late afternoon, the shadows
are perfectly placed, and I've used a wide-angle lens
to add an extra perspective to the shot, deepening the
blue sky and adding some depth to the old walls of
the church.
Camera: Canon EOS1; lens: 20–35mm; film: 50asa Velvia;
exposure: 1/400@f5

◄ It is nearly impossible to pass through southern France in February and not see at least one barren vineyard. The Tour Mediterranean is the ideal way to do this, and the dark trunks act as a perfect foreground for a peloton awakening from winter hibernation.
Camera: Nikon F5; lens: 80–200mm; film: 100asa Provia; exposure: 1/500@f5

► There are not too many street scenes that can be classified as landscapes, but there is something about this shot of the Tour Down Under in the seaside resort of Glenelg that is striking. Perhaps it is the depth of the crowds, intently awaiting a glimpse of the stars amassed for the race, or maybe it is the intimacy of the last minutes of the evening sun, managing to illuminate the backs of the riders before making an exit.
Camera: Nikon F5; lens: 80–200mm; film: 100asa Provia; exposure: 1/320@f4

►► The Étoile de Bessèges follows on from the G.P. Marseillaise. The five-day tour travels roughly east to west from the Marseille area to the former mining town of Bessèges. Invariably it crosses the old bridge near Cabriés, a few kilometers shy of another photographer's delight, the Aqueduc de Roquefavour. If the sun is shining, it is impossible to drive over the bridge without stopping to capture an image or two, as the glowing stone walls of the bridge and church seem to challenge the effervescent color of the cyclists crossing its span.
Camera: Nikon F5; lens: 28–70mm; film: 100asa Provia; exposure: 1/500@f5.6

► When you are 12,000 kilometers away from home, and only four days onto Australian soil, the sight of Aldinga Beach in South Australia is a sight to behold. And that's even before the Tour Down Under races past. The Southern Ocean is an almost unbelievable opaque blue at this time of the year, which allows the contrasting colors of the peloton to have their own influence in this shot. Each year the race does a three-lap stage around the McLaren Vale wine area, taking in Old Willunga Hill as well as the beach. It's a great chance to take three different shots, but this is the one that works best.
Camera: Nikon F5;
lens: 80–200mm;
film: 50asa Velvia;
exposure: 1/400@f5

▶ Another view of
Andalucía on a climbing
road between Nejre on
the coast and Jaén in the
1997 Ruta del Sol. This
shot is made more
interesting by the bright
yellow jerseys in the
foreground and the
strong shadows of the
cyclists on the road. Of
course the snowy peaks
in the far background
complete my enjoyment
of this scene.
Camera: Nikon F5;
lens: 20–35mm;
film: 100asa Provia;
exposure: 1/500@f5.6

▶ There's only one thing nicer than seeing a packed peloton squeeze through a line of plane trees in the Étoile de Bessèges: a big escape group racing through at 30 miles per hour! This is the 2001 race, on a stage between La Ciotat and Septèmes-les-Vallons where the wind has forced an echelon of riders ahead of the main group. Again, it is the direction of the sun that makes this image work— a horizontal light casting small spotlights on each tree trunk and sending exquisite shadows from each bicycle across the road.

**Camera: Nikon F5;
lens: 80–200mm;
film: 100asa Provia;
exposure: 1/500@f5**

► When I first went down to the Vuelta a Murcia, in 2001, I was expecting to see a boring landscape of near-desert attraction. Instead, I made one of the most startling discoveries of my cycling career: Murcia has as much to offer the landscape photographer as Spain's two most attractive regions, Andalucía and Cantabria. I was particularly taken with the sky at that time of the year, a deep, deep blue with evocative strips of cloud, all seemingly a few hundred meters above my head. Murcia is also a massive fruit-growing region, and March is when the apple blossoms are at their best—a sign of an early springtime compared with northern European countries.

Camera: Nikon F5;
lens: 20–35mm;
film: 50asa Velvia;
exposure: 1/320@f5

◄◄ This is the bumpy road between Motril and Cabra in Andalucía, during the 1997 Ruta del Sol. The olive groves are so vast and stunning that you can hardly see the peloton as it crests a rise and heads into a white-walled village.
Camera: Bronica ETRs; lens: 75mm; film: 50asa Velvia; exposure: 1/500@f5.6

◄ The palm trees at Seppeltsfield were in my sights again when the 2004 Tour Down Under passed through on its way to Kapunda in the second stage. Like so many other landmarks in my season, it is impossible to not try to get a shot of this unique cycling landscape. By using an ultrawide lens, I managed to compose the trees in a differently from my first-ever shot of these same trees in 1999—but only just!
Camera: Nikon D2H; lens: 12–24mm; digital image rated 200asa; exposure; 1/400@f6.3

SPRING

Printemps, primavera, voorjaar . . . Spring. For many people, and certainly for me, spring is the season of hope. It's a time when we look to the opening skies and sigh in blessed relief that winter is, finally, over. Then we look to the ground and note with delight the first buds of daffodils and crocuses.

◄ Beyond the far eastern side of Lac Leman, the town of Aigle stands at the foot of the beautiful Col des Mosses, where snowcapped mountains await the ever-keen photographer. But before we get that high, there is a landscape impossible to ignore: the combination of the peloton, barren vineyards, and the distant peaks above the Portes du Soleil.
Camera: Nikon F5; lens: 28–80mm zoom; film: 50asa Velvia; exposure: 1/320@f5.6

▲ The Giro d'Italia offers countless landscapes, yet this is one of the most unusual ones I've discovered in any country. We are on the eleventh stage of the Giro in 2003, and travelling through an extraordinary area they call Valli di Comacchio on the Venetian side of Italy. This shot would have been impossible had I not discovered an old lighthouse at the northern end of the causeway. The keeper allowed me to climb up the rusty ladder and onto the roof of the lighthouse, and I immediately made him close the front door to any other hopeful race photographers.
Camera: Nikon F5; lens: 300mm; film: 50asa Velvia; exposure: 1/350@f5.6

And if there's a lilt to our step, it's from hearing the forgotten sounds of chaffinches and larks, as they twitter cheerfully in unison at the turning of a cold and dreary season into what is, perhaps, the happiest season of all. Surely it's a happy time for followers of cycling, for spring is when the long months of uncertainty and inactivity are put to rest, new teams and new faces emerge onto the serious racing calendar, and the first big races start to occur. The landscape photographer enjoys this season best, too, relishing the most colorful months of the year, from the dying embers of yellow mimosa in mid-March to the glacial snows capping the green-treed Dolomites in late May, from Paris-Nice right through to the Giro d'Italia.

But spring is also a most challenging time, for the photographer as well as the racers. In events that promise rich rewards, the racing is of the highest caliber, and I have to fight for my place in my *own* quest to capture epic images. Each race becomes a blur of energy, in which I feel pulled at any given moment by battling desires: to record a momentous race crash or to paint the perfect picture postcard.

◄ Paris-Nice arrives each March on the Promenade des Anglais in Nice and ends with a circuit race for the entertainment of the tourists and residents of this cosmopolitan Mediterranean city. The wealthiest live or eat and drink at the Hotel Negresco, and they can look down on the race as it speeds past the hotel and its ornate flowerbeds still containing fresh mimosa. But it is a tricky shot to get: standing among the carefully manicured flowers just long enough to get the shot and moving on before the local police head your way!
Camera; Nikon F5; lens: 20–35mm; film: 50asa Velvia; exposure: 1/320@f5.6

that take up most of April and a few lonely days in October. The routes these races cover are as old as the roads themselves, reflecting the 100-year history of cycle sport in certain parts of Europe. Of course, this adds another challenge to the ambitious cameraman, since routes that barely change from one year to the next make it harder and harder to find compelling landscapes—new ones, that is. We know that the sea cliffs will watch over Milan–San Remo every year, just as the Mur de Huy will carry the climbing specialists to glory in the Flèche Wallonne. And we know that the Côte de Saint-Roche will offer the single greatest image of

◄ ◄ One of the all-time classic racing images is the spectator-packed climb of the Mur de Huy in a race called the Flèche Wallonne. A week or so after the Flemish classics in the north, it is time for the French-speaking Belgians to cheer on their heroes. Easy, thanks to three ascents of the hill with an average gradient of 19 percent. It is impossible to resist this same image each year, so I climb up onto the television scaffolding, plead with the cameraman for access to his privileged vantage point, and then fire away with an extremely wide-angle lens year after year. This particular shot was taken in 1999.
Camera: Nikon F5; lens: 20–35mm zoom; film: 100asa Provia pushed to 200asa; exposure: 1/250@f4

◄ The Côte de Saint-Roche is a typical dramatic-looking climb of the Liège-Bastogne-Liège race in southern Belgium. Located in the tourist Ardennes town of Houffalize, the climb is a natural congregation point for thousands of people on a Sunday morning, affording race photographers an early masterpiece just 85 kilometers into the event. Occasionally, we knock on people's doors to ask for a better vantage point—their bedrooms—but this cannot be done every year! Standing on the back of a motorbike is an adequate solution.
Camera: Nikon F5; lens: 80–200mm; film: 100asa Provia; exposure: 1/320@f4

▲ Limburg is the remote region of the Netherlands where the Amstel Gold Race is run each and every year. It being springtime, the fields are alive with color and the race has the added blessing of sun at its back. I always try to get at least one landscape that shows this pretty area at its best. Of course, it is probably more beautiful (and quiet!) without the bike race and its entourage of teams and fans. **Camera: Bronica ETRs; lens: 75mm; film: 50asa; exposure: 1/500@f5.6**

Liège-Bastogne-Liège a few days later, as surely as the quaint windmill at Beek will be the scenic highlight of the Amstel Gold Race. So the question we face annually is whether to shoot those same evocative scenes or drive right by in search of fresh material. Choose the latter and you may be considered original . . . or be castigated by your editors for not getting the quintessential shot. It's a tough decision.

In some ways, though, these ancient routes *have* changed, but not in ways pleasing to the landscape photographer. The increased use of cars and campers by spectators at the races, and the steady reparation and expansion of roads and buildings—all in the name of modernization—have somewhat tarnished our "traditional" images. Years ago, I spotted a new footbridge over a cobblestone path near the town of Orchies, a strategic point on the route of Paris-Roubaix. In those days I was not *in* the race on a motorbike, but would cut across the

◀ In a land famous for its number of windmills, it is surprising that there is just one along the many roads of Holland's Amstel Gold Race. It comes just after the village of Beek, 20 kilometers into the race, and it is the one single must-have shot for a landscape-hungry photographer each and every year. This is the best view in my opinion—taken with a long lens in order to overstate the size of the windmill in comparison with the cyclists.

Camera: Nikon F5; lens: 300mm; film: 100asa Provia; exposure: 1/400@f6.3

countryside to reach various vantage points along the course. That's how I discovered the footbridge. Then, as the race wound its way below the bridge, I took a shot, not particularly remarkable, which I recently had turned into a commercially available poster. One of the attractions of this image is the old, dilapidated, moss-covered farmhouse alongside the path, with adventuresome fans clambering onto its shaky roof for a better view. Go back to the same site today and you can no longer record that image. The farmhouse has been renovated and whitewashed to the point that my horizontal record of 1984 can now only be captured as a vertical shot—that is, if one can successfully crop out the new, huge superstore cruelly built on the once-exquisite horizon.

Modernization has brought significant changes to cycling race routes all over the

► The Tour of Flanders has started in Bruges for about six years now, and it is a vastly more photogenic experience than St Niklaas, where the race began for the previous 20 years or more. It is hard to find new angles each April when the race leaves town—this is a shot from the starter's platform in the middle of the "Grote Markt." The flags and gothic architecture add to the image, as does the murky early-morning light coming straight into the camera. This is a big occasion, the calm before the storm.
Camera: Nikon D2H; lens: 10.5mm fisheye; digital images rated 200asa; exposure: 1/250@f4

► You won't find this shot on any postcards of Belgium. This is the Het Volk race, traditionally held on the first Saturday of March and subject to the vagaries of northern European weather patterns. Surprisingly, it hardly ever rains at Het Volk; therefore, this shot, taken on the Oude Kwaremont, is a little bit more interesting than if it had been dry. I like the bleakness of this image, especially the way the cobblestones shine out of the gloom.

Camera: Nikon F5; lens: 300mm; film: 100asa Provia pushed to 400asa; exposure: 1/250@f3.5

world, and its effects are painfully evident in Belgium and France where the majority of the spring races are held. The landscapes of Paris-Roubaix have been hurt the most, with rural land cut up to make way for the high-speed TGV and Eurostar trains that crisscross the Pas-de-Calais near Lille. Meanwhile, in Belgium, local councils have finally succumbed to the inevitable, allowing many of their cobbled hills to be repaved, in order to present their villages in a better light. This is the price that's been paid for the ever-growing popularity of the Tour of Flanders classic. So the climbs of the Koppenberg and the Muur at Geraardsbergen are now more gently cobbled, turning them into mere shadows of their former selves. True, these landmarks are not literally "landscapes," but the cauldron-like Koppenberg, with its steep sides and 10,000 screaming spectators, has always been one of the sport's most atmospheric

▲ One of the delights of Paris-Roubaix is the sight of cobbled tracks without a single living soul upon them. I indulge myself each year by going over the entire stretches of pavé a few days before the race, familiarizing myself with the route and where the "best" cobbles are to be found, while taking the opportunity to capture their solitary beauty. The silence and peace of this area of France are something that Paris-Roubaix fans, in the tens of thousands, will never fully appreciate. I love these reconnaissance days every bit as much as the race days.
Camera: Nikon F5; lens: 20–35mm; film: 100asa Provia; exposure: 1/125@f5.6

images. As for the Muur, it seems that this hill has become such a popular tourist attraction that the town of Geraardsbergen had no option but to modernize it. Again, and ironically, thanks to cycling!

Back in the mid-1980s, when I first began this lifestyle of travelling and taking pictures, the racing calendar distinctly marked the transition from April—an often cold and barren month in Europe—to the warmer, more verdant May, with the Spanish stage race, the Vuelta a España. Sufficiently happy to experience six one-day classics in March and April, I would always pass up the end-of-April Amstel Gold to cover the Vuelta instead.

Spain in late April was indeed glorious, with its vibrant landscapes changing color and character almost daily, as the coattails

▶ The walled city of Ávila welcomes the 1994 Vuelta a España. The city is reached by way of the Puerto del Navalmoral, which is 30 kilometers away. I was following the leading group in this stage when I spotted the striking ramparts on the horizon—at which point I abandoned any ideas of photographing the finish and instead took shots from behind the group as they climbed the cobbled hill into Ávila. It works best with a bigger group of cyclists, but it is still a breathtaking landscape to have in one's possession.
Camera: Bronica ETRs; lens: 75mm; film: 50asa Velvia; exposure: 1/500@f5.6

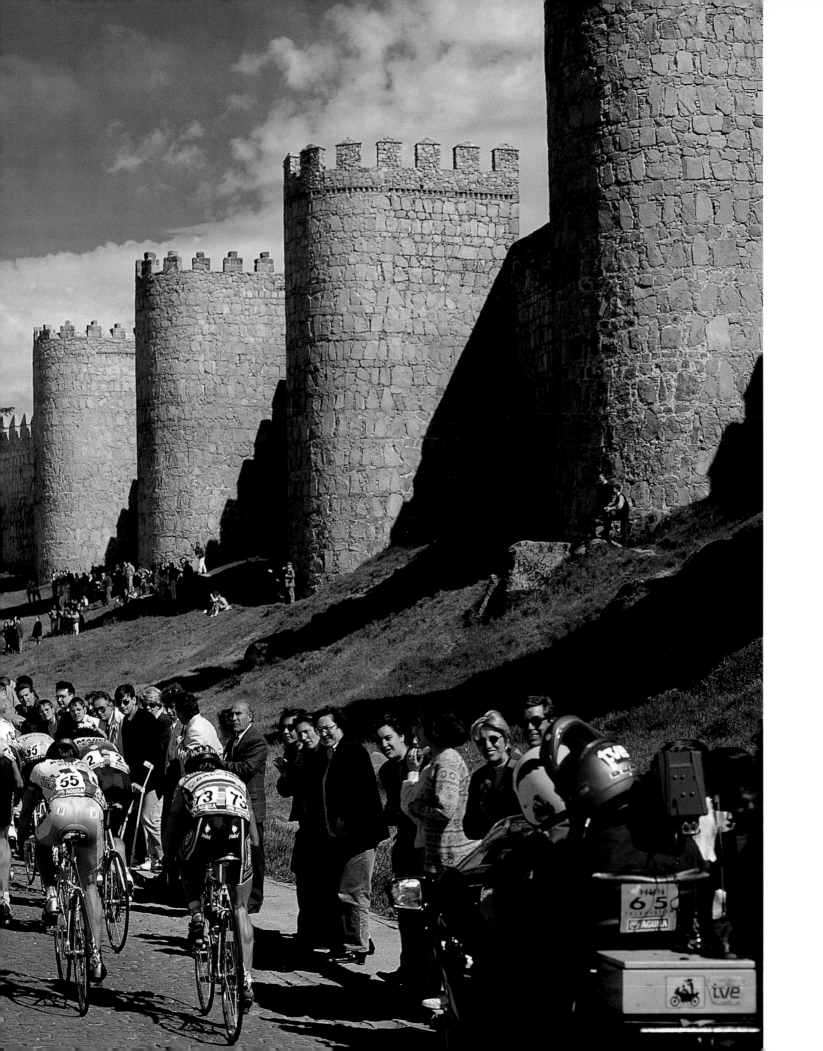

of winter dwindled away on the high plains. Yet the weather was still unpredictable enough that you could be travelling on a motorbike in shorts one morning, only to have to dive into a friendly race follower's car that afternoon to avoid snow or hail. This phenomenon provided me with some of my favorite landscapes, showing snowy peaks, lush green valleys, clouds, sun, and rain—often all in one image!

But the race calendar changed in 1995, moving the Vuelta to September and allowing the windmill-enhanced Amstel Gold Race to get more attention. Now, it is the Tour de Romandie that carries us gently from April into May, and what a beauty it is! Switzerland is Europe's prettiest country, a fact confirmed by the masses of tourists that flock there each summer and winter. Fortunately, they are *not* there in springtime, at least not where *I* choose to go, the northwestern part of the country alongside the French border. There, in the hills above the lakes of Neuchâtel and Geneva, you can find the true but still-secret beauty of Switzerland, in an area so unpopulated that cowbells are the only sound that disturbs the tranquillity. This is the French-speaking part of the country, a land of bucolic pastures, in contrast to the jagged mountains of German-speaking Switzerland. The mountain passes here are not the imposingly high Sustenpass or Furkapass, but the more gentle and romantic-sounding Col des Mosses or Col du Pillon. And instead of the hectic Zurichsee with its plethora of motorboats, you have Lake Geneva, where paddle-steamers still manage to operate in the old-fashioned way, beneath a huge tapestry of bare vignes.

Finally, to help us complete our celebration of spring, the Giro d'Italia beckons in the second week of May, fresh from its shift in the international calendar to allow cyclists the possibility of racing both here and in the Tour de France. A week earlier than it used to be, the Giro has inherited the fickle weather of the old Vuelta, while presenting a very different choice of landscapes. But what Spain offers in terms of vast open panoramas, Italy more than rivals with its ancient towns and villages like Matera in the south, Cava de Tirreni near the Amalfi coastline, and a teasing sniff of Assisi in central Italy. Nonetheless, unlike the Vuelta—where an entire stage can be raced with few signs of civilization or distractions—the Giro has

◀ We are in Gruyère, it is a peaceful morning, the sky is blue, the ground is alive with color, the mountains are still covered in snow . . . I feel I am in paradise. This was the scene following the start of a stage of the Tour de Romandie in 2000—an eye-catching setting even for someone like myself who has travelled in Switzerland so many times.
Camera: Nikon F5; lens: 20–35mm; film: 50asa Velvia; exposure: 1/320@f5.6

▶ I've been to the Amalfi coastline only once, but I can tell you that it is one of the most beautiful coastlines in the world. This image was taken during the 1997 Giro d'Italia on a stage that wound its way south from Pompeii to end up at Cava de Tirreni, close to Salerno. This is Praiano, but all of the dozens of small villages along this road are equally stunning—it was just a question of knowing which one to stop at, as there was no way we'd ever get past the strung-out peloton again on such a twisty road.
Camera: Bronica ETRs; lens: 75mm; film: 50asa Velvia; exposure: 1/500@f5.6

to venture to more extreme areas to find the remoteness and terrain needed for its legendary stock of mountain climbers to get to work. Decent landscapes are therefore harder to locate, and are often restricted to parts of the Apennines like Gran Sasso, to the Abruzzo mountains south of Tuscany, or to the little-known Piemontese mountains, with climbs such as the Agnello, the Fauniera, and Colle di Sampeyre. That is, unless the race ventures into the Dolomites, a veritable landscape paradise that is at its greenest and most beautiful in spring.

◄ A few hundred kilometers north of Venice is the range of mountains referred to as the Friuli Dolomites. It is here that the 2003 Giro d'Italia first used a previously unknown mountain called the Zoncolan. Fortunately for me, race leader Gilberto Simoni launched a solo break, giving me the opportunity to photograph him to within a few kilometers of the summit's finish line and then find this lookout over the mountain pass. Beyond are the Dolomites and more leg-burning climbs.
Camera; Nikon F5; lens: 28–80mm zoom; film: 50asa Velvia; exposure: 1/320@f5.6

74

◀ Global warming or not, it's been more than ten years since Paris-Nice last saw snow along the hilly roads behind Nice. This shot, taken in the mid-1980s, shows the peloton strung out along the Col de Vence on its morning run into Nice, with the uninhabited village of Courségoules contributing to this eye-pleasing landscape.
Camera: Nikon F3; lens: 135mm; film: 100asa; exposure: 1/500@f5.6

◀ The 2003 Giro d'Italia descends the Portella Mandrazzi to afford me with a wonderful view of Mount Etna on the island of Sicily. In moments like this you pick your location purely on instinct because you have no idea whether there is a better view later on. It is not as simple as stopping at the first place you find, but more a guess as to where the descending road is going, how the light will change accordingly, and whether this side of Etna is more photogenic than the other side.

Camera: Nikon D1X; film: digital, rated 200asa;
exposure: 1/400@f6.3

▶ This is not the most flattering portrayal of Segovia's famous aqueduct, but it shows just how much the waterway dominates the center of this beautiful city. The 1988 Vuelta a España is leaving Segovia on its final stage to Madrid. The aqueduct is so enormous that it is extremely difficult to photograph it in a way that doesn't completely lose the presence of the peloton. However, here I've made the peloton as much a part of the image as the aqueduct itself—you also get to see the tatty street signs and cluttered avenue full of parked cars and other distractions.

Camera: Bronica ETRs; lens: 75mm; film: 50asa Velvia; exposure: 1/500@f5.6–f8

▶ Barletta is a beautiful old Puglian town on the Adriatic coast that hosted a stage start of the 1995 Giro d'Italia. You cannot discover a place like this and not fall in love with it. And, as with most forms of love, it is a wrench to up sticks and leave town . . . even for a race as beautiful as the Giro.
Camera: Bronica ETRs; lens: 75mm; film: 50asa; exposure: 1/500@f5.6

◄ The first stage of the 2004 Paris-Nice passes beneath this magnificent aqueduct at Etampes on its way across to Montargis. We used to see this same view in the older Paris-Tours that started from the center of Paris—but I've never experienced the incredible lighting, which makes this shot more striking.
Camera: Nikon D2H; lens: 70–200mm; digital image at 200asa; exposure: 1/250@f4.5

► This is an image that partially explains the attraction of seeing the Vuelta a España in springtime. The race is climbing the Puerto del Navalmoral in 1994 as the rain begins to plunge from the clouds onto a group of cyclists struggling in the searing heat. The Sierra de Guadarrama can be seen in the background with the winter snow still far from completely melted . . . a photographer's delight!
Camera: Bronica ETRs; lens: 75mm; film: 50asa Velvia; exposure: 1/500@f5.6

► Italy is a country with churches, cathedrals, or simple chapels on every meter of road—or so it seems. But they are not all as grandiose or photogenic as this one in the hilltop town of Osimo in the region of Marche, and not all benefit from the passage of the Tirreno-Adriatico stage race. I used to speed across to that side of Italy during the night, hours after the last stage of Paris-Nice, to catch the last few days of Tirreno—a 600-kilometer journey made worthwhile by a single image such as this one.
Camera: Canon EOS1;
lens: 28–80mm;
film: 50asa Velvia;
exposure: 1/320@f5.6

▶ The Provençal village of Bonnieux towers over the Paris-Nice peloton in 1998. Again, the sun lifts the color of the cyclists perfectly, and illuminates in equal capacity the stone walls of houses and cottages stacked into the hillside. The camera flatters this scene, for when you get closer to the village, the masonry and walls are a lot less picturesque than they appear from afar.

Camera: Nikon F5; lens: 80–200mm; film: 100asa Provia; exposure: 1/500@f5.6

▶▶ The Col du Pillon was the scenic highlight of the 2003 Tour de Romandie, which took place after a very wet winter that left meters of snow on even the lower Alpine peaks. This was a one-chance shot, as the peloton soon broke into smaller groups on this steep climb. I took my chance before the climb really began, which helped.

Camera: Nikon F5; lens: 28-80mm; film: 50 asa Velvia; exposure: 1/500@f5

▶ The 1996 Tour DuPont remains the only USA-based race I've ever photographed—not including the Olympic Games that same year. I enjoyed the Appalachian mountains enormously, and the quaint Virginian landscapes were something to behold. But this image of the peloton racing past a church in North Carolina took my eye even more, though I am not sure if it is because of the lens I used or the puffy white clouds in an otherwise clear blue sky.
Camera: Canon EOS1; lens: 16mm fisheye; film: 50asa Velvia; exposure: 1/500@f5.6

► The ancient bridge
over the Rio Sinca is
found alongside the road
that leads to Huesca,
and on to Zaragosa, as
shown here in a stage
of the Vuelta a España.
We were descending
the Pyrenees with the
previous day's ski-station
finish at Estación Cerler
fresh in our minds. The
bridge acts as a sort of
gate between the greenery
of the mountains and the
parched, windblown
desert of Aragon. While
it requires a short but
tricky rock climb to gain
the necessary vantage
point, this shot proves
that it is a worthwhile
pursuit.

Camera: Nikon F3; lens:
180mm; film: 100asa;
exposure: 1/250@f5

▶ This one image adequately tells the world just what a pretty country England is. Trouble is, it also serves to warn everyone about the fickle weather awaiting them. This is Lancashire, 275 miles north of London, and more specifically, the Trough of Bowland. Luckily, the bad weather passed over us before the Tour of Lancashire arrived on the climb, and the sun came out to afford me this most delightful image of England in springtime.

Camera: Nikon F3; lens: 135mm; film: 100asa; exposure: 1/500@f5.6

► This is now a regular landscape in my seasonal wanderings. We were in the Tour de Romandie in 1999, on a stage toward Lausanne, and I discovered a tiny lane climbing up into the vineyards that gave me a breathtaking view over Lac Leman and the peloton, with the Valais mountains close on the horizon. A few years later the Tour de France passed this exact same point, and the vines were a deeper green. But with the stage finish so close, I couldn't risk stopping—something that is not so difficult in the more relaxed Romandie race.
Camera: Nikon F5; lens: 80–200mm zoom; film: 50asa Velvia; exposure: 1/320@f5.6

►► The Vuelta a España on the French side of the Pyrenees? Yes, it happens every once in a while—this was in 1995. We are heading toward the Col d'Aspin, before passing over the Peyresourde and Portillon cols on our way back into Spain. I love this shot, a carefully composed one that emphasizes the might of the mountains and the antlike peloton—a longish lens has added to the illusion.
Camera: Nikon F4; lens: 300mm; film: 100asa; exposure: 1/250@f4.5

◄ The countryside around Charleville-Meziers is quite remarkable, yet there are always some nice scenes to be found when the Critérium International comes to the region each March. I found this scene purely by chance one morning, just as the peloton was warming itself up under the weak sun. Even the car and motorbikes lend a great deal to this peaceful image.
Camera: Nikon D2H; lens: 300mm; digital rated 200asa; exposure: 1/500@f6.3

► Until a few months before this shot of Paris-Nice was taken on Mont Faron, there was a forest of trees that blocked out all views over the city of Toulon and the Mediterranean, and it had been that way for as many years as anyone could recall. Then came the summer fires of 2001, which destroyed the trees clinging to the steep cliffs and opened up the hill to some stunning panoramics. In fact, Mont Faron has a prettier side offering more diverse landscapes, and Paris-Nice used it one year later, but the view of the naval base of Toulon is still breathtaking on a clear day.

Camera: Nikon F5; lens: 28–80mm zoom; film: 100asa Provia; exposure: 1/320@f5

▶ The 2004 Critérium International begins to wind up its pace in the second stage as the mist clears away in the French Ardennes. This is such a rare image—capturing the March light—and I spent the rest of the weekend delighted with what I'd found in the north of France, along the banks of the Meuse River. **Camera: Nikon D2H; lens: 12–24mm zoom; digital rated 200asa; exposure: 1/320@f5.6**

► Because the Oude Kwaremont comes early in the Het Volk race, it is an obvious location to shoot a landscape before the serious racing really starts. The fact that it is raining and miserable only helps this image, and we can see the day's struggle beginning to show on the riders' faces. I'd prefer it without the spectators in the background, but in some ways they add another dimension to the landscape.

Camera: Nikon F5; lens: 300mm; film: 100asa Provia pushed to 400asa; exposure: 1/320@f4

In 2003, the Paris-Nice race climbed the Col d'Eze for the first time *en ligne,* and gave us some new landscapes overlooking the Mediterranean Sea. There had nearly always been an individual time trial up the same hill, but as a group the images were far more interesting, especially since the stage was held under warm sunshine and blue, blue skies. Camera: Nikon F5; lens: 80–200mm zoom; film: 50asa Velvia; exposure: 1/320@f5.6

▶ The 2004 Giro d'Italia went over a Dolomite pass I'd
never before seen—the Passo di Falzarego. It is a quite
unique climb with a short tunnel that takes the riders up
to the final three kilometres and a series of zig-zag ramps
to the top. Unfortunately for me, the Saeco team of
Gilberto Simoni and Damiano Cunego was chasing an
escape group really hard, and the peloton was in a long,
thin line—not what I wanted. But the result is pleasing
enough, all the same.

Camera: Nikon D2H; lens: 105mm fisheye; digital image
rated 200asa; exposure: 1/500@f8

▶ This is Paris-Nice on one of its more gorgeous days in the south of France, climbing through the morning mist toward the ancient village of Gourdan in 1988. In those days, there were two stages on the final leg. The morning's jaunt was La Mandelieu to Nice, starting early enough to ensure some superb lighting conditions, making this a very moody shot.

Camera: Nikon F4; lens: 85mm; film: 100asa; exposure: 1/500@f4.5

► While this image looks like the middle of a very serious climb in the Dolomites, it is actually a picturesque road in the far south of Italy, not far from the city of Taranto, one of Italy's main naval bases. The flowers give a hint of the season and act as the perfect foreground to this Giro d'Italia landscape.
Camera: Canon EOS1;
lens: 28–80mm;
film: 50asa Velvia;
exposure: 1/400@f5.6

SUMMER

É*té, estate, verano* . . . Summer. With its abundance
of sunshine, this is the season that heightens our
good humor, sense of well-being, and desire to
go on holiday—a factor that brings millions of
people to the roadsides each July to watch the
Tour de France.

But for me, summer means June and the Dauphiné-Libéré stage race. Also held in France, this weeklong event takes place exclusively in the area surrounding the Rhône Valley, with a northern point no higher than Lyon and a southern reach to the Haut-Var. Three things are guaranteed here: beautiful weather, to-die-for scenery, and a hearty taste of what summer means to the French. For the first time since Paris-Nice in March, we experience Provence again, but now gussied up with seasonal festivities in every town and village the race

◀ I felt as if I was actually in the peloton when I took this shot of the 2003 Dauphiné-Libéré on the beautiful Col du Lautaret. A fisheye lens has given this impression, but I am actually just a few inches away from the cyclists in order to get the might of the mountains in as well. There's a heavenly quality to this image—not least because we are up at about 6,000 feet—but there is also the intensity of the cyclists as they power their way up the climb at the start of a very tough day.
Camera: Nikon D1X; lens: 16mm fisheye; film: digital, rated 200asa; exposure: 1/320@f6.3

▶ The Tour de Suisse passes through Ulrichen on its three-pass epic in 2002. This is a dream of a landscape, discovered from a point about five kilometers up the Nufenenpass, which allows us to look down on the tiny peloton as it passes through this ancient timbered village. When your day starts with a view like this one, you know it is going to be great.
Camera: Nikon F5; lens: 300mm; film: 50asa Velvia; exposure: 1/320@f5

◄ The Dauphiné-Libéré takes place at that early time in the summer when there are still some decent snows to be seen on the mountaintops. In 2001, there was more snow than anyone expected, and the few photographers who bothered to attend this charming race were blessed with a dozen great landscapes. This is a shot taken on the climb of the Col de La Croix de Fer, and it is enormously enhanced by the cloud that gives a teasing view of the distant snow. In the background is the road branching off to Col du Glandon, another legendary alpine cycling climb.
Camera: Nikon F5; lens; 80–200mm; film: 100asa Provia; exposure: 1/320@f5

▼ The Passage du Gois is a causeway out on the Morbihan peninsula in the far west of France. It is usually covered by the sea, except at low tide. The Tour de France crossed the road in 1999, but the organizers misjudged the timing of the tide and the race arrived so early that the road was still wet and slippery in places, and as a result crashes were tenfold. The crashes and the wind broke the peloton into echelons, and I chose the perfect observation platform to watch their effect on the racing. Lance Armstrong and his teammates are at the front of this broken peloton, wreaking havoc on their rivals and taking another step toward securing Armstrong's first Tour victory in 1999. I doubt if the Tour will risk crossing this ocean road again, so it makes this an even more poignant landscape to me!

Camera: Nikon F5; lens: 300mm; film: 100asa Provia; exposure: 1/500@f5

visits. A wine tasting here, a game of bowls there . . . and beret-clad old men seeking shelter from the sun under a canopy of trees in Cavaillon, where they sit smiling and chatting with animation. It's as if the Dauphiné-Libéré heralded the official arrival of the holiday season. In fact, it does: summer.

Even before the race takes us up the high mountains of the Haute Savoie, our busy lenses are taking in landscapes adorned with fruits of the earth. Rows and rows of grapevines that were brown in March are now a deep, glowing green on the banks of the Rhône at Tain L'Hermitage, or along the considerable flanks of Mont Ventoux. Fields of pale lavender, still shy of their deep-purple midsummer hue, entice us with their soft beauty and fragrance, as we

travel through valleys that contain still more of Provence's delights: the exquisite villages of Gordes, Apt, and Bonnieux that so inspired Peter Mayle's *A Year in Provence* back in the late 1980s.

The Dauphiné carries us to towns like Digne-les-Bains and Sisteron, where we notice *les gitans,* those gypsy travellers who lend their charisma to the bars and cafés whose tables clog the narrow sidewalks. Meanwhile, the streets are clogged with British, Belgian, and Dutch tourists, driving through on their way to the beaches of the Côte d'Azur, their worldly possessions strapped precariously to the too-small roofs of their Opels, Renaults, and Rovers. And finally, the race reaches its climax for the racers *and* photographers, on the snow-clad peaks of the French Alps. Now that, to me, is what summer in France is all about.

▼ The 1995 Dauphiné-Libéré climbs toward the summit of the 6,000-foot Col du Galibier. This was quite a unique shot, as I'd never before seen the Galibier with so much snow. The cloud gives the image a distinctly claustrophobic element and actually benefits my photography as it subdues the light a little, allowing us to see both the cyclists and the stacks of snow on the roadside, which might have proved impossible if the sun had been shining.
Camera: Canon EOS1; lens: 16mm fisheye; film: 100asa Provia; exposure: 1/500@f6.3

◄ Italy's summer usually arrives after the first week of the Giro d'Italia, and helps to bring out even more *tifosi* than ever. This is the Colle di Agnello, in the 2000 Giro, and I've gone for a shot that tries to show the size of the crowds near the summit of this beautiful peak in the Piemontese Alps. Ironically, what really makes this image are the wispy clouds being blown over the peaks behind the race and the trace of winter snow.
Camera: Nikon F5;
lens: 16mm fisheye;
film: 50asa Velvia;
exposure: 1/500@f5.6

This was a chance photo, taken on a stage of the Tour de France from Mégève to Alpe d'Huez in 2003. I was ahead of the race looking to have a pee and instead found this group of farmers waiting to greet that 100-year-old Tour. Dressed in their typical Savoie outfits and with their horse and cart fully rigged up, they make an idyllic image.
Camera: Nikon F5; lens: 28–80mm; film: 50asa Velvia; exposure: 1/250@f4.5

Take your choice: the Col du Galibier in the Dauphiné or the Col du Galibier in the Tour de France. A *petit* peloton climbing between green meadows where the only "intrusion" is the masses of yellow and red flowers, or a *grand* peloton worming its way up the same climb, but hidden from view by a 5-kilometer-long row of campers parked before the summit. In the Dauphiné's climb, both beauty and grandeur are on display. Only grandeur is evident in the Tour's ascent six weeks later.

Yes, the Tour's immense and growing popularity has a distinct downside: The views that everyone comes to see are no longer there. As a result, the Dauphiné seems ever more

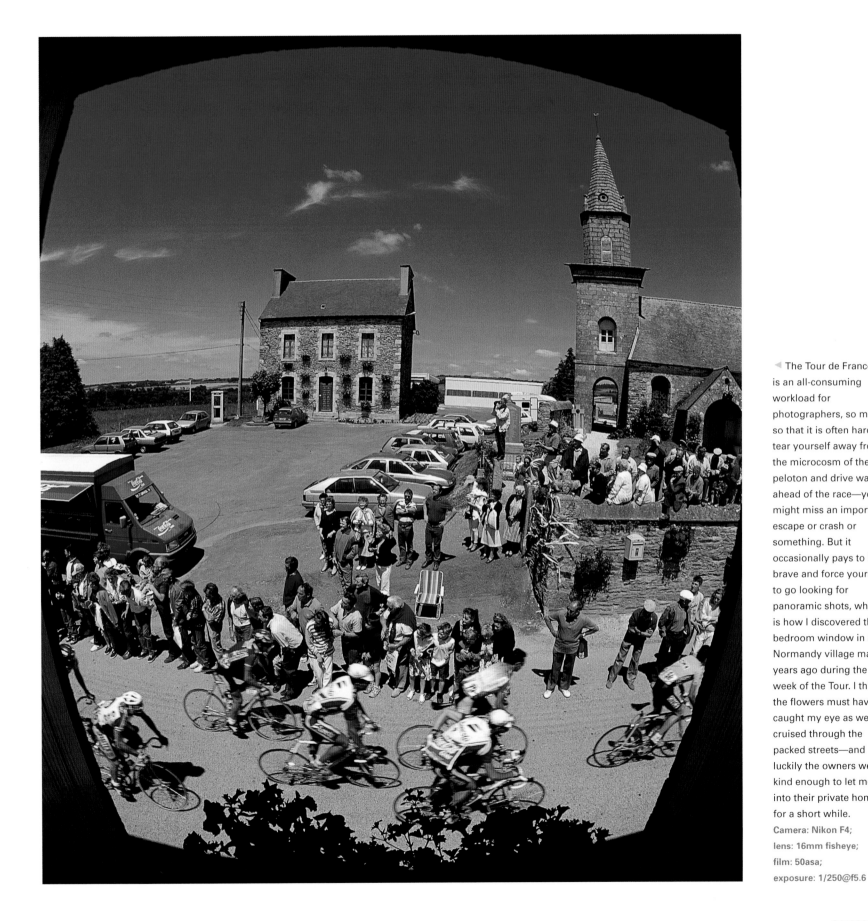

◄ The Tour de France is an all-consuming workload for photographers, so much so that it is often hard to tear yourself away from the microcosm of the peloton and drive way ahead of the race—you might miss an important escape or crash or something. But it occasionally pays to be brave and force yourself to go looking for panoramic shots, which is how I discovered this bedroom window in a Normandy village many years ago during the first week of the Tour. I think the flowers must have caught my eye as we cruised through the packed streets—and luckily the owners were kind enough to let me into their private home for a short while.
Camera: Nikon F4;
lens: 16mm fisheye;
film: 50asa;
exposure: 1/250@f5.6

enjoyable. In 2003, I stood on a switchback about 8 kilometers from the summit of the Galibier, at the point on this northern face where the *real* climbing begins. With no fans in sight, a most beautiful vista opened before my eyes as the leading riders made their way up, led by Lance Armstrong and Iban Mayo, with the Pic de la Moulinière as a masterful backdrop. The image was good, though not good enough, for the tiny group was just that—too tiny. So I vowed to return to this site in the Tour, when a bigger group would fill the foreground more lavishly.

Over one month later I tried to do just that: find the exact same piece of road with its overlook to the zigzag course below. But my task was impossible. It was as if I were on another mountain pass altogether. Not one section of road seemed the same as before, and the view across to La Moulinière was transformed by hordes of people, cars, and vans.

A sad experience, yet one that made me appreciate even more the Dauphiné, where each year I discover an Alpine wonderland unspoiled by signs of humanity and just begging to be photographed. It's been that way since I first saw this race back in 1991, when I was left breathless at the sight of Les Gorges de la Bourne on a stage from Orange to Villard-de-Lans.

◄◄ The old Peugeot race car gives a clue to the age of this image: 1987. We are on the Col du Galibier, just at the point where the Meije Glacier can be seen at its mighty best, and where I've put myself following a reconnaissance made one week before the Tour de France began. The landscape is so striking that the car really doesn't spoil the view at all—and the multicolored peloton more than drowns it out anyway! There are so many views one can get from the Galibier climb, but you get only one good one each time. I think this is one of my favorites, probably because it was one of my first.
Camera: Nikon F3: lens: 135mm; film: 100asa; exposure: 1/500@f5

▲ Burgundy or Champagne? More than fifteen years after this image was taken in the 1989 Tour de France, I cannot be sure whether we are looking at a stage to Reims or a stage to Dijon. In any case, it is a typical view of the Tour in summertime, with spectators' camper vans along the grassy shoulders and everyone seemingly enjoying a picnic while the race comes past. Judging by the small size of the peloton, we might even be looking at a stage in the Tarn, or the Alsace, perhaps after an ascent of the Ballon d'Alsace.
Camera: Nikon F4; lens: 300mm; film: 100asa; exposure: 1/500@f4

Another year it was the novelty of experiencing the unsurfaced last few kilometers of the Col du Coq. And the greatest highlight for me came in 1995, on the southern side of the Galibier where the race was virtually entombed by massively high banks of fresh snow. I felt totally alone up there in the clouds, watching respectfully and in awe as the brave band of cyclists pedaled their way to the 6,500-foot summit, seemingly unaware of the dangers—and imposing beauty—of their surroundings.

Only one other race can compete with the majesty of the Dauphiné, and ironically it's the race that follows it by just a few days: the Tour de Suisse, set a few hundred kilometers away and showcasing the Swiss Alps. As a race, the Tour de Suisse is just

▶ This is an imposing shot of the Giro d'Italia climbing toward the Passo di Gardena in 1993, with the Gruppo di Sella mountains as a dramatic backdrop. Beauty aside, this shot is interesting because of the cyclists at the front of the race. Men like (left to right) Guido Bontempi, Stefano Allocchio, Alessio DiBasco, Mario Cipollini, and Giuseppe Calcatterra were the "heads" of the Italian cycling scene back then, and they controlled the pace at which this stage started—with three or four major passes to climb. More importantly, we photographers have to be nice to them on days like this in order that we may pass, pass, and repass the peloton on the Gardena Pass— for my money, Italy's most beautiful climb.
Camera: Bronica ETRs; lens: 75mm; film: 50asa Velvia; exposure: 1/250@f5.6

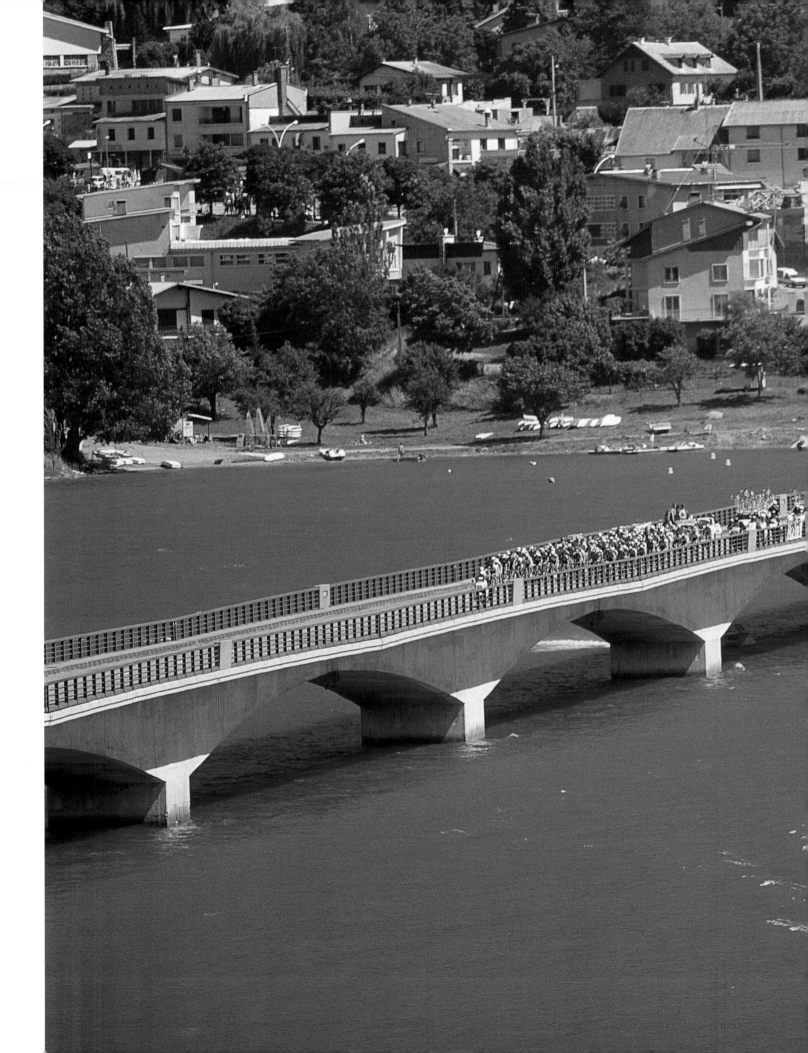

◄ The Lac de Serre-Ponçon is a stunningly beautiful reservoir to the east of Gap, a southern gateway to the French Alps. The Tour first crossed it in 1996 and I managed to discover its potential while I was well ahead of the race—something that can be pretty hard to do in the modern Tour de France. Thankfully, the sun was high in the sky and as a result, the water is more intensely blue than usual. Of course, without the speedboat this shot might be a lot less appealing.

Camera: Canon EOS1;
lens: 300mm;
film: 50asa Velvia;
exposure: 1/500@f5

▶ This is a shot of the drug-blighted 1998 Tour de France crossing a brand-new bridge over the Durance River in the Alps. Bridges and cyclists do not always go well together in photography, as their dimensions are completely opposite! But the use of a fisheye lens has distorted the image to the point that the cyclists—and in particular Marco Pantani's yellow jersey—make up at least 50 percent of the image area.
Camera: Nikon F5;
lens: 16mm fisheye;
film: 50asa Velvia;
exposure: 1/500@f5.6

The 2002 Tour de Suisse, travelling from Meiringen to Meiringen. We are now on the Grimselpass, a phenomenal climb that speaks legends for the skills of Swiss engineers who built such a difficult road years ago. To then construct a dam and create Switzerland's highest reservoir only adds to the spectacle. Sadly, the cyclists weren't empathetic to my art on this occasion— racing almost from the first kilometer to the point where only a thirty-man group was left on the Grimselpass. A landscape like this requires at least a 100-man peloton to balance the alpine splendor.

Camera: Nikon F5; lens: 80–200mm; film: 50asa Velvia; exposure: 1/320@f5.6

Italy has so many picturesque regions, and each one is so distinctive from any other, that it is impossible to say which one is the nicest. This is what appears to be an aerial shot of a hilltop village somewhere in the Abruzzi mountains near Rieti, in the 1993 Giro d'Italia. It was fortunate that there happened to be a strung-out line of cyclists in the village streets, because I would have taken a shot of this place anyway! There is nothing quite like the excitement of looking down on a climb such as this and watching the race inch its way so slowly toward you. In case you haven't guessed, I am not in a helicopter or plane, but standing on the same road that those same cyclists must continue climbing up . . . which is why I like the Abruzzi so much.

Camera: Bronica ETRs; lens: 75mm; film: 50asa; exposure: 1/500@f5.6

There are absolutely no cyclists at all in this image taken on the Col d'Izoard in 1989. The little piece of mountain carries a monument to two of the sport's greatest cyclists—Louison Bobet of France and Fausto Coppi of Italy—erected after both men died in the 1960s. The monument is found along the road that runs through the Cassé desert, after the climb of the Izoard is over. It is accessible from either France or Italy—meaning that whenever the Tour de France or Giro d'Italia passes this point, Bobet and Coppi are remembered by today's cycling champions.

Camera: Bronica ETRs; lens: 75mm; film: 50asa; exposure: 1/500@f5.6

▶ Cardiff is one of the most historical cities in the United Kingdom, but I never truly appreciated it until Kellogg's Tour of Britain ended a superb stage there in 1987. The organizers risked a lot by ending the stage right in the middle of Cardiff's famous castle—and on its cobblestone road! This was one of several landscapes featured; it shows a little of the race and a lot of the history of that day.

Camera: Nikon F4: lens: 24mm; film: 50asa; exposure: 1/500@f5

▶▶ England first organized a World Cup race in 1990, which was based in Brighton and provided quite a party atmosphere the whole weekend—a culture shock for the hundreds of European cyclists and followers who traveled across the English Channel! There were several landscapes to choose from, with the South Downs being the most obvious. But I preferred this unusual shot of Brighton itself, complete with the holiday fanfare and the famous Palace pier.

Camera: Nikon F4; lens: 28mm; film: 100asa; exposure: 1/500@f5.6

It is September 11, 2001, and I am standing above a beautiful reservoir called Embalse del Porna, 80 kilometers inland from Gijon. I had been there a good ten minutes before the race, but became furious when a rival photographer's motorbike suddenly parked itself right in the middle of *my* precious landscape! I felt my shot had been ruined by this, and spent the next hour cursing silently to myself at how selfish some people are . . . and then the news from New York broke on the race radios. Suddenly my problems seemed totally feeble in comparison with the tragic victims of the terrorist attacks, and I quickly forgot all about the messed-up photograph. This is *my* personal memory of where I was when the Twin Towers fell—a million miles away, both geographically and spiritually.

Camera: Nikon F5; lens: 28–80mm;
film: 50asa Velvia; exposure: 1/320@f6.3

◄ ◄ If I were to take this same shot today, from the same position on the Passo Mortirolo as I had in 1991, I doubt that I would be able to see any of the road at all because the crowds that line this monstrous hill in today's Giro d'Italia are now so massive the whole way up the climb. In 1991, there was hardly anyone there at all, and the little chapel has a dignity and importance all its own. Look closely at the four cyclists in the shot—their body angles give away the fact that the Mortirolo is an extremely steep ascent to make, which is why it is so popular with today's cycling fans.
**Camera: Bronica ETRs;
lens: 75mm;
film: 50asa;
exposure: 1/250@f4**

◄ The Nufenenpass in central Switzerland has many points along its 15 kilometers where one can capture a wondrous landscape. This is the 2002 Tour de Suisse on a stage that took in three such monster climbs; this was my second landscape of the day, and I was already on my second roll of film— it felt great!
**Camera: Nikon F5;
lens: 28–80mm;
film: 50asa Velvia;
exposure: 1/320@f5**

◀ Like most of the sport's one-day races, the Clasica San Sebastian follows pretty much the exact same route every year, making it a challenge for photographers to find original images. Even so, there is always something new to be found, such as this view over the Bay of Biscay, at a point in the race where the road turns inland at Garate and climbs into the hills. Here you get an idea of just how pretty the Basque coastline is, with its sheer rocky cliffs and pounding surf. It's no wonder that someone created a sprawling cemetery there hundreds of years ago. What a great place to rest in peace.
Camera: Nikon F5; lens: 300mm; film: 100asa Provia; exposure: 1/250@f5

◄ ◄ There was a time, not so long ago, when my post–Tour de France summer was dominated by the Kellogg's Tour of Britain. Here we are in the southwest, passing through Winchester on a balmy summer's day—like the older established Milk Race, this was an excuse to see a country I'd hardly ever experienced, as most of my career has been spent in continental Europe.
Camera: Nikon F3: lens: 180mm; film: 100asa;
exposure: 1/500@f4

◄ Way back in 1986, I followed the Tour de France in a car, one year before ascending in grateful stature to an in-race motorbike. But using a car gives you a fantastic opportunity to choose the best spot each day, and specifically a chance to find pretty towns like Pont-Audemer in Normandy. It can be hard work to knock on doors and beg people to let you use their upstairs rooms for your photography, but the results can be quite satisfying. And you know those motorbike-borne photographers will never get close to images like this.
Camera: Nikon F3; lens: 180mm; film: 100asa;
exposure: 1/250@f4.5

▶ Less like a landscape, more like a shot of a cyclist crossing a bridge in Dinard. But this image, taken in a time-trial stage of the 1989 Tour de France, constitutes a landscape for me, so appealing is the typical Normandy architecture of this tranquil fishing village. I've been waiting for an excuse to publish this shot for years!
Camera: Nikon F4; lens: 28mm; film: 100asa;
exposure: 1/500@f5.6

◄ Normandy competes with Brittany to lay its claim as France's home of cycling. Certainly Normandy is more heavily populated, and its towns and villages can produce a bigger crowd when the Tour de France passes through— such as here in Fougères, in the 1990 Tour. Just as in Brittany, there are a dozen great cycling champions who hail from Normandy, and Fougères lays claim to three of them: Albert Bouvet, Robert Mangeas, and Alain DeLange.
Camera: Nikon F4;
lens: 85mm;
film: 50asa;
exposure: 1/500@f5.6

◄ The Clasica San Sebastian rolls out of town a bit too early to catch the thousands of sun-worshippers who flock to the beach in the late morning. But we still feel obliged to capture this image each August because this summer classic's race will take many hours to get fully under way and we need something to record of the first few hours of the race.

Camera: Nikon F5; lens: 16mm; film: 50asa Velvia; exposure: 1/320@f5

▼ Not your typical cycling landscape, is it? This is the 1999 Tour de France, on a stage to Thionville, exactly one year after the scandalous Tour that almost ruined the sport for good. It seems that summer brings out the fun in almost everyone, and the Tour becomes a regular target for exhibitionists. I know the cyclists hate shots like this—they regard it as a rude gesture, disrespectful in every sense. But scenes like this make for fun images and I couldn't resist stopping to capture this unique, and cheeky, moment. But, I'm glad I was on this side of the camera!

Camera: Nikon F5; lens: 28–80mm; film: 50asa Velvia; exposure: 1/250@f5.6 with flash

◄ The stunning Passo del San Gottardo in southern Switzerland, which hosted a stage finish on its summit in the 2001 edition of the Tour de Suisse. I've used a fisheye lens to bring a different perspective to the shot— I knew the race would be completely fragmented after a long day in the mountains and there would be little chance to fill the foreground with a nice fat peloton. The high sun becomes a feature as well, making this quite a balanced landscape.

Camera: Nikon F5; lens: 16mm fisheye; film: 50asa Velvia; exposure: 1/500@f5.6

◀ Even the center of London gladly closed its streets to host the final of Kellogg's Tour of Britain in 1986. On a circuit that took in Trafalgar Square, the Embankment, and the Houses of Parliament, I was well and truly spoiled for a choice shot!
Camera: Nikon F3: lens: 24mm; film: 100asa; exposure: 1/500@f5.6

◄ Until the mid-1990s, England hosted a round of the World Cup competition, with the city of Leeds being the host site because of its proximity to the hills of Yorkshire. Holme Moss was the favored viewing point for thousands of fans who had never seen the likes of Lance Armstrong, Johan Museeuw, or Laurent Jalabert performing "live." The fact that the race passed twice here made it a great location for the race photographers as well.
Camera: Nikon F4: lens: 28mm; film: 100asa; exposure: 1/500@f5.6

▶ The mid-1990s were the heyday of British cycling fandom. In addition to the Tour of Britain, we hosted the Tour de France in 1994, with two stages in the south. This is the leg that went from Portsmouth to Portsmouth, passing through delightful English villages like Westfield. Knowing the real Tour would start only once we were back in France, I wanted to make sure I had something that showed the race among thousands of excited fans—more than you would normally find along the roads of France.

Camera: Canon EOS1; lens: 35–70mm; film: 100asa; exposure: 1/250@f4

One of the things a Tour de France photographer has to do each evening is study the race manual for photo opportunities the next day. One evening in 1991, I noted the name of Honfleur on the race route, and asked the opinion of a journalist friend, John Wilcockson, if this village was as pretty as its name suggested. "Yes," he said, "it is beautiful." . . . So I made sure to be well ahead of the stage and discovered Honfleur in good enough time to pick the best location. I persuaded a family to let me climb to their fourth-floor bedroom in order to get the vantage point I needed to record this image of the peloton ambling gently past the fishing port. This is a once-in-five-years type of shot.

Camera: Bronica ETRs; lens: 75mm; film: 50asa; exposure: 1/500@f5.6

AUTUMN

*A*utomne, *autunno, otoño* . . . Autumn. Yes, it has its golden moments, but beneath that transient glow, autumn remains the most melancholy season of the year. It's the time when we notice that the sun's rays are weakening, evenings are growing chillier, and there is less and less daylight available

171

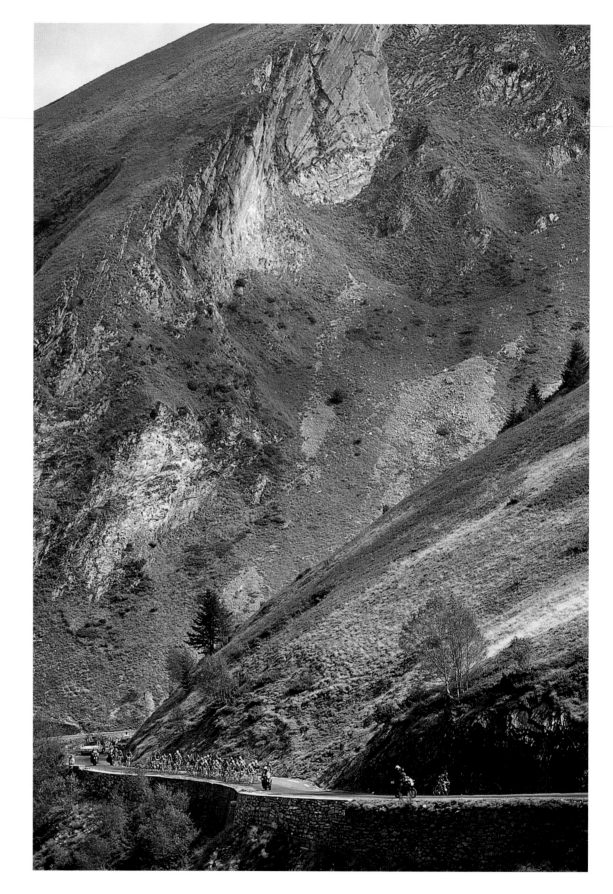

◄ The town of Amboise is a popular tourist attraction along the Loire Valley. It is also the single most attractive point between Paris and Tours—France's last one-day classic of the year. Like many other landmarks in cycling, the chateau above the town cannot go unphotographed each October. I once tried a different shot by paying seven euros to enter the chateau and shoot the race from above, but it is still the shot from the bridge that works best.
Camera: Nikon; lens: 20–35mm; film: 100asa Provia; exposure: 1/500@f5

► This is the Col d'Aubisque in September, a complete contrast to the same mountain that we knew so well in July. The Vuelta a España made this climb on its way back into Spain, following two French stages in 2001. I particularly like the autumn colors that paint this mystical mountain in a different light altogether.
Camera: Nikon F5; lens: 80–200mm; film: 100asa Provia; exposure: 1/500@f4.5

to enjoy. With sadness, we realize that winter is just a few bike races away, and the balmy days of summer will soon be nothing more than distant memories. Yet as surely as autumn is the lovers' choice for romance, it's also a favored time for cycling photographers, who look forward to that warm, gentle light on the horizon, as we try to eke out a few more weeks of pleasure on the racing circuit. And we milk it for all we can, knowing that we'll soon be immersed in a long winter, with no real racing in sight for many months.

It's difficult to say exactly when *my* autumn begins, since September's Vuelta a España somewhat lessens my awareness of summer's end. But even in Spain, even in the southern

▲ The countryside around Zaragoza seems to be a landscape of an earlier century, with giant sand walls dominating the skyline and adjoining many of the Vuelta a España routes. The wind has shaped these formations over the years, and the same wind wreaks havoc with the Vuelta peloton on this particular day, making this a nicely composed image.
Camera: Nikon F5; lens: 80–200mm; film: 100asa Provia; exposure: 1/500@f5.6

▶ The Vuelta a España climbs into high Andalucía on a
stage in 1996, with a picturesque village as a backdrop
for some ferocious racing that day. With the absence
of green olives and snowy peaks, it was nice to capture
at least one landscape in this region.
Camera: Canon EOS1; lens: 70–200mm; film: 50asa Velvia;
exposure: 1/500@f6.3

deserts of Andalucía and Murcia, it's hard not to notice the sun setting that much earlier. The spectators are the ones who most blatantly give it away, appearing at the roadsides with their anoraks or sweaters toward the end of the afternoon. Meanwhile, the cyclists are also responding to the cooling temperatures, donning arm-warmers in the first hour of racing if we're in the mountains of Asturias or Cantabria and scrambling for their warm down jackets at day's end, even in the still balmy center of the country. The weather can turn nasty, too, for the first time in months. And there's nothing quite like a freezing cold downpour to wash away all memories of summer, as you abandon, at least temporarily, any hopes of finding a decent landscape under leaden skies and a wet northerly gale.

▲ The Lake of Lecco looks better with sun shining on it, but I still like the mood set by this image, taken at the 1989 Giro di Lombardia.
Camera: Nikon F4; lens: 135mm; film: 100asa pushed to 200asa; exposure: 1/250@f4

Certainly, the Vuelta now playing in September is not the Vuelta that used to inspire me so when it took place in April and May. Gone are the snowcapped mountains and luminous green pastures of the Pyrenees or the Sierra de Guadarrama, north of Madrid. Instead, there's a certain sameness in the climate and terrain. This can mean a frozen landscape devoid of surprise or color, parched land that hasn't seen rain for some time. Andalucía is the region most dramatically changed since February's Ruta del Sol. Back then we saw fields of rich, dark brown soil from which Seville's famous oranges grow. Now the bright white crystallized land is begging for some respite from the dryness. Yet if you venture out onto the high plains around Ávila and Segovia just as the sun starts to weaken at five o'clock, you can see Spain in another

◄ The Vuelta a España passes through Asturias, a wonderful region of Spain, as often as it can to attract tourism. The pearl of the region is Lagos de Covadonga, nestled below the Picos de Europa mountains. In fact, I took this shot the next day, as the Vuelta raced back down to the sea at Santoña in Cantabria. The shot works only because of the fisheye lens, which has distorted the winding road and offered an acceptable contrast to the strong backlighting.
Camera: Nikon F5; lens: 16mm fisheye; film: 50asa Velvia; exposure: 1/500@f6.3

▲ Aragon is one of Spain's most parched regions, especially in September following months without rain. I was drawn to this barren landscape in the Vuelta a España on a stage to and from Zaragoza, with the race spread all over the road thanks to the strong winds that always prevail in that area. It is definitely a landscape characteristic of the Vuelta in early autumn.
Camera: Nikon F5; lens: 80–200mm; film: 100asa Provia; exposure: 1/500@f5.6

light, literally. It is there and then that the ground—bleached by months of summer sun and near-drought conditions—turns golden, as if in final, stubborn resistance to the changing seasons. That the stages of today's Vuelta end at around six o'clock adds to the attraction of photographing this lit-up landscape of awesome mystery.

Any doubts as to whether autumn has begun are brutally cast aside in the first week of October, when we arrive in Paris for the final sprinters' classic, Paris-Tours. Even when graced with a warm, peloton-slicing, southwesterly wind, this race definitively announces that it's time to cover up those bare suntanned arms and legs and dig into your wardrobe for a thermal undervest. Fortunately, this is only a one-day event and there's a real possibility of warmer times in the Giro di Lombardia two weeks hence, for northern France in October can be a shock to the system after three weeks in Spain, with a temperature change of about

◄ Since the open frontiers policy of the European Community was adopted, Spain is probably the single country within the union that has had the most *autopistas* built. Happily, they take traffic off the smaller roads and allow us to enjoy thoroughfares like this in the province of Cuenca. This is the Vuelta a España in 1999, on a stage to Guadalajara, and I've traveled for about 20 kilometers along this stretch of road before settling on this landscape, which relies heavily on the towering cliffs to the right. But again, it is the line of cyclists that really completes the picture. What the camera cannot show is the exceedingly bumpy road they are racing over—the cyclists must wish they were racing on one of those *autopistas.*

Camera: Bronica ETRs; lens: 75mm; film: 50asa Velvia; exposure: 1/500@f5.6

► A most typical view of Paris-Tours, this image is usually among the first frames of the day after the race has pulled away from its starting point in St. Arnoult-en-Yvelines. But very few of these images actually work because a bit of luck is required to get such a perfectly composed line of trees and a complacent peloton into one frame. It's nice when it does work, though!

Camera: Nikon F4; lens: 135mm; film: 100asa; exposure: 1/500@f4

ÀRD FHIONÀIN
ARDFINNAN →

CAISLEÀN NUA NA SIÙIRE
NEWCASTLE 4½

6. AN CLOICHÍN
CLOGHEEN →

TUAIN MEALA 8

25 degrees Fahrenheit. Nonetheless, Paris-Tours offers such a splendid contrast in landscapes that you soon feel ready to forget all about the Vuelta.

One of the most striking images you'll find here is centered on people rather than terrain. True, there are long avenues of plane trees soon after the start in St. Arnoult-en-Yvelines, followed by wriggly, rolling roads that take the race across a somewhat bleak plateau in Eure-et-Loir. And it's hard to forget the almost hypnotic sight of the peloton splitting into so many fragments because of the wind. But France in October means the official start of the long-awaited hunting season, and as photographers, we hunt out a landscape dominated by men in oilskin coats and hats who bear sturdy rifles on their shoulders and hide their bloody catch in leather pouches tied to their waists. This may not be an image to frame and hang proudly on your office wall, but it *is* unique and eye-catching. The men have no doubt been hunting

▲ One has to hope that Ireland will never change, no matter how much the pro-European influence forces it to reform some of its novelties and tradition. This is a typical scene near Carrick-on-Suir in 1989.
Camera: Nikon F4; lens: 28mm; film: 100asa; exposure: 1/500@f5.6

► The 1998 world's was held in Limburg, an exceedingly beautiful region in the south of Holland. The amateur race was held under sunny conditions, and the windmill on the circuit at Margraten provided us with a race landscape at the modern-day championships.

Camera: Nikon F5; lens: 80–200mm; film: 100asa Provia; exposure: 1/500@f5

▲ I found these two hunters about 80 kilometers into Paris-Tours in 2000, after looking for what seemed like hours. It is not the prettiest location or the prettiest image, but we photographers have to take our chances when and wherever we can.
Camera: Nikon F5; lens: 20–35mm; film: 100asa Provia; exposure: 1/250@f5.6 with flash

since dawn, and they were seen in greater numbers when Paris-Tours began its southern march at a much earlier hour—back in the days when the race was a full 300 kilometers long. But if you wait patiently, now and again—though not every year you'll spot a group of hunters who are postponing their return to the pub just long enough to catch the passing of this autumnal classic.

Since 1996, October has also been the month for the world road championships, held in different countries each year all over the globe. Yet whether these races highlight the windmills in Limburg, the castles in Spain, a legendary motor-racing circuit in Belgium, or an

The 2000 world championships in Plouay provided me with a surprisingly decent landscape, but it is interesting only because of the long, long lens I've used to create this intense image of the peloton passing through the packed start/finish area.
Camera: Nikon F5; lens: 500mm; film: 100asa pushed to 200asa; exposure: 1/320@f5

impressive suspension bridge across the Tejo River in Lisbon, the chances of capturing a classic cycling landscape have been greatly reduced. It's not just that the locations are bland, and it's not because the regions are lacking in heritage—far from it! It is the sheer impossibility of viewing the races without also viewing the ugly metal crowd barriers encircling the entire course. They may well be a modern-day necessity to protect such an increasingly popular sport, but they do nothing for the image of cycling as a free, roaming theater on wheels, a carnival whose participants are utterly heroic in their chosen quest for glory. All the more reason to herald the beautiful Giro di Lombardia, coming just one week later.

The "Race of the Falling Leaves" has followed many different routes throughout the years, with starts at Como, Milan, Monza, Varese, and now Como again. But wherever it starts, it always leads to the beautiful lakes of northern Italy and allows us, for one last time, to experience that indescribable pleasure of blending cycling and scenery in a timeless image . . . as long as the sun is shining. There can be no better end to a working season than a Giro di Lombardia blessed with crystal-clear skies, vistas of snowcapped peaks across the Alps, and deep blue lakes to send us, almost in a trance, to Bergamo and the finale of this great race. I recommend spending a second day in Lombardy, preferably along the shores of Lake Como, in order to appreciate all the more the splendid beauty of this region and to soak up the postrace, postseason tranquillity with a glass or two of Nebbiolo red wine.

Of course, our search for cycling landscapes can extend for a much longer time, taking us to cyclo-cross events, six-day races, or even the Caribbean—where cyclists can't resist at least one more race if it takes place under warm, tropical conditions. But a long winter sabbatical offers a chance to replenish our appetite for the months of travel that lie ahead, and to recharge our minds and senses so we are once again ready to absorb all that we see and compose new, wonderful cycling landscapes.

There's really nothing quite like it, this obsession with landscapes and cycling. It's a world apart from any other, one that constantly reminds me how lucky I am to be involved in such a great adventure.

▶ Today's Giro di Lombardia climbs the Madonna del Ghisallo early in the day, and as such we get to see a composed peloton and a stunning Lake Como bathed in sunshine . . . unless it is rainy, in which case you can see nothing of the lake. But this is the only panorama of the day that shows such vistas—a disappointing contrast to the old days when the race made three or four excursions along the lakeshores. Following Lake Como is the chapel of Ghisallo, which gives the hill its name. We have to scurry away before the peloton gets to us in order to get a decent vantage point and record one of Italy's most revered shrines to cycling and cyclists, both dead and living.
Camera: Nikon F5; lens: 80–200mm; film: 50asa Velvia; exposure: 1320@f5.6

◄ I took this image of the Vuelta a España in 2002, forfeiting a shot of the stage finish in order to capture one of my favorite scenes: the entry of the main group into Ávila's walled city. I'd been here before, many times, and knew exactly where to place myself as the race turned off the normal roads and onto the brutal cobblestone climb. But it wasn't as easy as this back in 1985, when I'd stumbled across this same view just by chance and got only a grabbed shot that barely did justice to the splendor of this town. Ávila competes with its neighbor Segovia and the equally ancient Toledo for the title of Spain's most beautiful city.

Camera: Nikon F5; lens: 28–80mm; film: 50asa Velvia; exposure: 1/320@f5.6

◄◄ This is the 2003 Vuelta a España descending an ancient road near to Collado Villalba on the third-to-last stage. This is one of many such roads now bypassed by more modern carrateras or autopistas—and we are better off for it!
Camera: Nikon D1X; lens: 12–24mm; digital image at 200asa; exposure: 1/400@f5.6

◄ Alcala La Real is a significant market town in central Andalucía. Its claim to fame is the magnificent castle sitting high above the town. The 2003 Vuelta approached the castle from the south with the sun making it that much more photogenic. The peloton merely adds something of human interest and color.
Camera: Nikon D1X; lens: 70–200mm; digital image at 200asa; exposure: 1/500@f6.3

► Like the majority of photographers, I probably spend many days a year cursing because the light is not where I'd like it to be. But sometimes the opposite is true, such as in this shot of the Vuelta a España passing the vast palace of El Escorial in 1999. It looked completely wrong when I first found the location, with strong backlighting certain to leave the shot underexposed with little foreground detail. But in fact, the silhouette of the palace is what sets this shot off—that and the multitude of shadows from the cyclists as they take a corner.
Only the policeman ruins this picture now.
Camera: Nikon F5; lens: 20–35mm; film: 50asa Velvia; exposure: 1/320@f4

◄ I could quite likely fill an entire book with images from the Tour of Ireland, a race that spanned nearly the entire careers of Sean Kelly and Stephen Roche, Ireland's famous cyclists of the mid-1980 to 1990 era. There wasn't one year when we didn't come across a gem of a view somewhere around the Emerald Isle. This is the 1986 race, and we are following a small escape group as it begins the climb of the Gap of Dunloe in the Kerry mountains. There are many elements that make this image a bit special: the clouds hovering on the mountaintops, the dirt road, the ominous horizon where the race must climb. But it is probably the bright yellow and orange jersey of the last cyclist that really illuminates this image.
Camera: Nikon F3;
lens: 85mm;
film: 100asa;
exposure: 1/500@f4

▶ This image is typical of a modern-day Vuelta a España and its sun-bleached hillsides where a thirsty peloton is already suffering under the fast pace of the race. We are in a part of Spain hardly used by the Vuelta—the Sierra del Cadi—north of Lleida on a very hilly, twisty trajectory to Andorra, where our day will finish with the monstrous climb of Arcalis.
Camera: Nikon F5; lens: 80–200mm; film: 50asa Velvia; exposure: 1/320@f5

▶▶ The Lake of Lecco is the twin of Lake Como, filling the River Adda with crystal-clear mountain water from the Alps. The view of the lake from the Colle di Balisio is probably one of the best there is—but it is made even more pleasurable by the inclusion of cyclists descending the mountain in the Giro di Lombardia.
Camera: Bronica ETRs; lens: 75mm; film: 50asa Velvia; exposure: 1/250@f5.6

► This landscape looks very Italian, when in fact it is northern Spain with the Vuelta a España racing past the Embalse de Tremp on its way to the Pla de Beret in the Pyrenees. Just as it looks Italian, it could also be mistaken for June because there is so much color in the vegetation and the crystal-clear waters. However, it is September, and therefore a pleasing landscape to offer.
Camera: Nikon F5; lens: 28–80mm; film: 50asa Velvia; exposure: 1/320@f5.6

◄ The Vuelta a España moved to a later date in 1996, and started in Lisbon, Portugal, for the first time in its history. We had to wait a few days to find out if Spain in September would be as photogenic as it is in the spring. In the meantime, I clocked this landscape along the way to El Estoral on the first stage.
Camera: Nikon F5; lens: 80–200mm; film: 50asa Velvia; exposure: 1/500@f5

◀ Memories of a great race come flooding back when I consider this image of the Tour of Ireland from 1988. I had to climb a long way up a boggy hillside to get this view over Connemara, but this image remains one of my all-time favorites. The end-of-season, early autumn light is probably what makes it so evocative, as well as the reflection in the glittering river.
Camera: Nikon F4;
lens: 85mm;
film: 100asa;
exposure: 1/250@f5.6

◄ This is the Col d'Aspin in France . . . but it's not the Tour de France! The Vuelta a España crossed over the famous climb in 2003, on its way back into Spain via the Col du Portillon. On this side of the Pyrenees there is still some strong color in the trees and hillsides, which makes this a somewhat idyllic image for early autumn. Note the lack of metal crowd barriers and ugly plastic signage that is an expected blemish on many Tour de France landscapes taken in this era.

Camera: Nikon D1X;
lens: 12–24mm;
digital rated 125asa;
exposure: 1/320@f5.6

▶ The first world
championships to be
held in October took
place in 1996. The
organizers were lucky to
have nearly summer
conditions in Lugano,
Switzerland. The bright
colors of the peloton
were still an attraction,
forming this landscape
early in the long race.
The lighting is crucial
here, creating a romantic
autumnal gem.
Camera: Canon EOS1;
lens: 70–200mm;
film: 100asa Provia;
exposure: 1/320@f5

▶▶ The great thing
about great champions is
that they are always at
the head of the peloton
when it matters the
most—such as here at
the Gap of Dunloe in the
1986 Tour of Ireland.
Sean Kelly is the man
making me happy as
he leads the way up
the gravel track to the
summit of this delightful
mountain near Kilkenny.
There's a stark beauty to
this image, the colorful
cyclists, the blue lake on
the horizon . . . and the
chilly-looking spectator
who ventured this far up
the mountain to see the
race. I bet he, too, was
thrilled to see Kelly at
the front.
Camera: Nikon F4;
lens: 85mm;
film: 100asa;
exposure: 1/250@f4

◀ In many ways it is difficult to consider this indoor shot as a landscape, but we can get away with it so long as we are talking about cycling landscapes. This is the velodrome in Munich's Olympic Park, which was used as a warm-up track for cyclists about to race in the 1976 Olympics on Munich's other, since-demolished, outdoor velodrome. Although the track looks tiny in this shot, it is in fact an illusion caused by the fisheye lens I had to use to get its oval completely into the picture. The track is used mainly for the six-days of Munich—one of the sport's most popular winter competitions.

Camera: Nikon F4: lens: 16mm fisheye; film: 100asa pushed to 200asa; exposure: 1/60@f4

► One edition of the Nissan Tour of Ireland made a stage based around the "Ring of Kerry," the splendidly beautiful region of southwest Ireland that juts out into the Atlantic Ocean. The ocean mist kept visibility to a minimum that day, but race followers still got a glimpse of the wonderful scenery.

Camera: Nikon F4; lens: 135mm; film: 100asa; exposure: 1/250@4

► Descending toward Galway Bay on a stage of the Nissan Tour of Ireland, this is one fine image of the race that brought world-class cycling to the homes of millions of Irish fans, and cemented the folklore of Sean Kelly and Stephen Roche. **Camera: Nikon F4; lens: 135mm; film: 100asa; exposure: 1/500@f5.6**

◄ The Giro di Lombardia is often referred to as the "Race of the Falling Leaves" because it takes place in October. This shot from 1989 is characteristic of the race's beauty—the peloton climbs the Esino Lario above the Lake of Lecco with the trees burning brown and gold and green.
Camera: Nikon F4;
lens: 135mm;
film: 100asa;
exposure: 1500@f4

◀ ◀ These trees made a superb backdrop for the seventeenth stage of the 2003 Vuelta, which ran through some pretty arid areas northwest of Madrid. I used a longer lens to accentuate the might of the forest over the miniscule peloton.
Camera: Nikon D1X; lens: 300mm; digital file at 200asa; exposure: 1/500@f5.6

◀ In the desert lands around Segovia, this is the Vuelta a España climbing into the Sierras for the last mountain stage of the 2003 race. It is hard finding decent landscapes in Spain in September, but once again the trees have added some color and interest. And again, the long lens has added depth.
Camera: Nikon D1X; lens: 300mm; digital images rated 200asa; exposure: 1/500@f6.3

INDEX

◀ Warm Irish lighting gives away the location of this shot of the 1986 Tour of Ireland as it climbs its way up Mount Leinster on a stage down to Cork. I spent most of my "Ireland" days leapfrogging the peloton to get images like this—three or four decent ones each day on average—and I was never disappointed with the results!
Camera: Nikon F4; lens: 24mm; film: 100asa; exposure: 1/500@f5.6

◄ This is the Vuelta a
España in 2003, on a
stage from Granada to
Cordoba. We were on an
interior road in Andalucía,
somewhere among the
olive groves near to
Antequera, and I spotted
the ruins of a castle,
which made it impossible
for me to pass without
taking a shot.
Camera: Nikon D1X;
lens: 70–200mm; digital
image rated at 200asa;
exposure: 1/500@f5.6

▶ Can you imagine this lot coming under your house in the morning? We are at the 2004 Giro d'Italia, a few kilometers north of San Vendemiano in the Province of Treviso, and the race is heading hard and fast toward the Dolomites. I can't be sure whether this is someone's house or an unused factory or watermill alongside a flowing river. Either way, it made for a satisfying early race image that day.

Camera: Nikon D2H; lens: 70–200mm; digital image rated 200asa; exposure: 1/320@f5.6

ABOUT THE AUTHOR

Graham Watson has traveled the world in pursuit of his love of cycling landscapes and this book is the culmination of nearly thirty years of imagery. Watson was born in the heart of London in 1956, but his chosen pastime and occupation is far removed from city life. Trained as a society photographer, Watson hit upon cycling in the summer of 1977 on a visit to the Tour de France. He immediately embarked on a life of discovery and adventure that is still paying dividends today.

Watson is author of numerous books about competitive cycling such as *Kings of the Road*, *Visions of Cycling*, *The Road to Hell*, and *Graham Watson: 20 Years of Cycling*; however *Landscapes of Cycling* is the first of his books to be solely dedicated to the varied landscapes that play host to the world of cycling.

Cor Vos